MEDITERRANEAN
MEAL PREP
COOKBOOK

Heart Healthy Recipe Ideas
for Cooking Ahead and Saving Time

Linda Gilmore

TABLE OF CONTENTS

INTRODUCTION

Are you looking for a diet that isn't just geared toward rapid weight loss? Do you want a diet that works to change your overall health and well-being? Do you want to start making changes to your diet that you will be able to maintain for the rest of your life? The Mediterranean diet works differently than other 'trendy' diets because it has been used by the population that inhabits the Mediterranean region and has been shown to have long-term health benefits such as longevity.

Fad diets often do not consider your overall health and instead focus on one specific goal—usually weight loss. However, they typically are not successful when looked at in the bigger picture because they are often extremely restrictive and not realistically maintainable over a long period of time. As a result, most people will quickly regain the weight they lost on a diet as soon as they start adding back in other foods that the diet restricted. On the other hand, the Mediterranean diet allows you to eat a wide range of foods, making it a great choice for a larger portion of the population. Anyone can find meals that they love that follow the Mediterranean diet.

This diet allows you to reach your health goals without compromising the taste of your meals. The Mediterranean diet gives you easy adjustments you can follow, and by reading this book, you are already taking the first step. This book will provide easy recipes you can prepare; in doing so, you may not even feel like you are on a diet!

I was never conscious of my health growing up. I had countless guilty pleasures and would always go for junk food when given the option. And I never felt good. But at the time, I didn't realize that my nutrition was at the heart of all the problems that I was experiencing. It was only when one of my college roommates started cooking for our shared apartment of three that I learned to love healthy foods. Her family was from Greece, and she was an excellent cook, especially for a college student. We would have roommate dinners, and I was introduced to cuisines I had never experienced. As I learned more about food, cooking, and nutrition, I started incorporating more of a Mediterranean diet into my daily life. That's when I noticeably started feeling better than I ever had. I lost some weight, but changing my diet was never really about losing weight as much as it was about feeling better physically and mentally.

Besides my college roommate, I didn't have many resources to help me learn about adapting my diet. Because of that, it took me a while to fully develop my eating habits, and I did so by trial and error. With this book, I hope to help you in your journey so that you can easily transition into your new diet and healthy lifestyle. I love the Mediterranean diet because it has truly changed my life. I have experienced first-hand how much making simple changes to your diet can change your physical and mental health.

MEDITERRANEAN LIFESTYLE

The Mediterranean Sea lies between 21 different countries, including countries from Africa, Asia, and Europe. Because of this, the diet in this region consists of an incredibly diverse array of cultural influences. Today, the "Mediterranean diet" typically refers to a diet based on cuisines from the regions of Spain, Italy, Greece, and Turkey.

Starting in the 1950s, researchers worldwide began studying the effects of different cultural diets on different populations' health. Specifically, heart disease became a common research point when studying alongside diets. During that time, Mediterranean populations showed significantly fewer heart disease signs. Later research on the topic has shown that the diets of the Mediterranean populations help with individuals' longevity and heart health, as well as other physical health benefits.

Once you start experimenting with the recipes in this book and find what kinds of foods are your favorites, you will want to eat these Mediterranean recipes instead of thinking about them as necessary for your diet. This is the major turning point in your diet journey because it's when it will begin to get easy. Starting a diet is always the hardest part because it will be slightly unfamiliar territory. However, finding a diet you love, just as I have, will tremendously relieve the burden.

The longer you wait, the harder it will get, as you will grow more rooted in any unhealthy habits you engage in, consciously or unconsciously. Because you have bought this book, you are already on your way to becoming healthier! The recipes in this book will give you the tools to continue your journey.

Adopting healthy cooking techniques is vital in your journey of taking on the Mediterranean diet. When you learn how to cook in healthy and fun ways, you can enjoy the act of cooking and eating the food you prepare.

Trust me when I say that your body will thank you. Here are some helpful tips regarding small changes you can make to transition into your new lifestyle.

- Allow herbs and spices to become your new go-to. This will help add flavor to your meals without adding too much salt. Experiment with different kinds of herbs and spices to use in your cooking.

- I also recommend making lower-fat substitutions where you can. Most foods nowadays have low-fat options. For instance, try to select a leaner cut when cooking with beef. When using dairy in your cooking, try to use a reduced-fat option. You can also easily replace butter with extra virgin olive oil in your cooking.

- The Mediterranean diet discourages foods high in unhealthy fats, such as trans fats and saturated fats. However, the diet does not restrict fat altogether. In fact, there are healthy fats—monounsaturated fats and polyunsaturated fats—that you can eat in the Mediterranean diet. Extra virgin olive oil, for instance, is a major staple in the Mediterranean diet that contains healthy fats.

ESSENTIAL INGREDIENTS FOR THE MEDITERRANEAN DIET

The typical Mediterranean diet includes vegetables, olives, grains, legumes, fruits, seeds, nuts, dairy, seafood, and poultry. Historically, these foods have appeared in abundance in the Mediterranean region, and the diet builds meals around these staples.

This diet is less about following a strictly restrictive regimen and more about making smarter choices with your eating habits. This makes the diet accessible and maintainable in the long term.

The people I have worked with on this diet have all been able to maintain it easily. They often tell me how surprisingly easy it is to keep up because they have so many go-to recipes that are quick, easy, delicious, and also healthy. Finding recipes you love is the key to succeeding with a new diet. Suppose you don't love what you're eating even more than what you were eating before starting the diet. In that case, you will constantly be tempted to return to your old, unhealthy eating habits.

Foods that can serve as staples in this diet include:

- vegetables
- fruits
- whole grains
- legumes
- beans
- seafood
- poultry
- avocado
- olives
- extra virgin olive oil
- herbs
- spices
- tomato sauce
- pesto
- balsamic vinegar
- dairy
- seeds
- nuts

Foods that you will want to avoid as much as possible include foods that are heavily processed, such as:

- processed sugars

- deli meats

- soda

- saturated and trans fats

- fast food

- Any foods with heavy additives (these are foods that can easily be identified by looking at nutrition labels. If you see lots of ingredients that sound chemically, unpronounceable, or unfamiliar, you will want to avoid them).

A NOTE ON EXTRA VIRGIN OLIVE OIL

Extra virgin olive oil is the least processed, natural form of olive oil, and it is always recommended that you choose extra virgin when selecting olive oil. It contains the most flavor as well as the most antioxidants and nutrients.

- When choosing olive oil to buy from the grocery store, look for the harvest date on the bottle. You will want to avoid it if it does not have a harvest date and only an expiration date. Try to buy the olive oil bottle with the most recent harvest date. It should also come in a darkened shade.

- It usually comes in either a dark green bottle or in a tin. You will want to avoid olive oil in a clear bottle. You will also want to store your olive oil away from heat and light. The pantry or cupboard makes for excellent storage space for your oil.

MEAL PREP BASICS

Meal prepping may sound intimidating for anyone unfamiliar with it. It can seem like a lot of work, but it actually doesn't have to be. Meal prepping simply allows you to prepare meals strategically to save you time, money, and food waste and also allows you to make more conscious eating choices. This can be a massively helpful tool for your diet journey. It will help you easily transition into your new lifestyle because it keeps you on track by giving you a concrete structure to follow.

Planning and preparing your meals ahead of time eliminates the burden of struggling to figure out what to eat at the moment when you are hungry. By having ready-to-go meals, you will know exactly what to eat, which will help stop you from grabbing a quick but unhealthy choice, such as a bag of chips or a candy bar. You will not have to worry as much about macros with meal prepping because that work is already done for you.

ORGANIZING AND STORAGE TIPS

1. The first step in changing your diet happens in the grocery store. Because of this, it is always a smart choice to plan ahead and make a grocery list of everything you need to buy to prepare your meals for the week. This will help you to avoid making impulsive purchases, and you will also avoid buying foods that do not follow your new diet, as well as overspending. It will also save you some time in the grocery store, as you will have a solid plan and know exactly what you are in there to buy.

2. Deciding what to purchase in the grocery store can be unhelpful and stressful. When I used to do this, I often spent a ton of money, only to come home and feel like I didn't have anything to eat. That was because I was not planning out my meals. I had a lot of food, but I did not have any meal plans. Consider what you want to cook for the week, and make your grocery list based on those meals.

3. Eating a meal or snack before going to the grocery store can also be beneficial. When you go grocery shopping while you are hungry, you will be more tempted to buy everything because everything will seem tasty to you at the moment. This does not help you stick to the plan, even if you do go to the store with your prepared grocery list. Having a full stomach at the grocery store gives you much more control.

4. Remember to keep the Mediterranean diet in mind at the grocery store. You will need to purchase food items other than what's on your planned meal prep list for snack foods. This can be an easy opportunity to stray from your diet. It can be quite tempting to pick up snacks you are familiar with, but they are not necessarily the healthiest options. Try to keep in mind the information you know regarding nutrition and the diet, and make your decisions based on this new knowledge. This will inform you what snacks you can have that align with the Mediterranean diet, such as fruits and nuts.

5. Most importantly, you will want to stick to fresh foods and avoid processed foods. Processed foods tend to contain high levels of sodium and processed sugars. When in doubt, remember to read nutrition labels, reading both the macros and the ingredients. By taking this extra step, you can easily avoid making unhealthy choices.

A NOTE ON STORAGE

Many of these recipes have a relatively large yield because they are geared toward helping with your meal prepping.

- You will want to separately store your dry and wet ingredients for these meals. For instance, many bowl recipes include a salad portion, a dip portion, a grain portion, and a meat portion. When preparing these bowls, you will make all of these portions separately and then combine them only when you create the bowls themselves. It is best to store all of these portions separately, and then once it comes time to eat, you will want to combine all of the portions together.

- For reheating your prepared meals, you can typically use a microwave. However, with the meals cooked in the oven, it is recommended that you reheat them in a toaster oven if you have one. You can also always use a stovetop to reheat any of your meals.

Remember that the Mediterranean diet is not a diet that is geared toward rapid results. It is focused on long-term success, so you should allow yourself some patience. Starting any diet will come with some challenges. Remember that everyone experiences this—you are not alone! *You have taken the first step in choosing to improve your overall health.*

NOURISHING BREAKFAST

POTATO HASH WITH POACHED EGGS

Serves: 4

Prep Time: 10 min.

Cook Time: 24 min.

NUTRITION FACTS (PER SERVING):

Calories: 535, Carbohydrates: 34.5 g, Protein: 26.6 g, Fat: 20.8 g, Sugar: 6.9 g

INGREDIENTS:

extra virgin olive oil

1 white onion (70 g), chopped

2 garlic cloves, minced

2 medium potatoes (340 g), chopped

salt

black pepper

1½ tsp. allspice

1 tsp. dried rosemary

1 tsp. Spanish smoked paprika

1 tsp. dried coriander

½ tsp. granulated sugar

4 medium eggs

1 tsp. white wine vinegar

1 red onion (70 g), chopped

1 bell pepper (120 g), chopped

½ cup (140 g) pepperoni, chopped

1 cup (60 g) fresh parsley, chopped

5 pickled cucumbers

DIRECTIONS:

1. Heat 1½ tablespoons olive oil in a large skillet over medium-high heat. Add your onions, garlic, and potatoes. Season with salt and black pepper, and cook for 5–7 min., often stirring, until the potatoes are tender.

2. Add pepperoni and bell peppers. Season with salt and black pepper and the rest of your spices. Cook for 5–7 min. Reduce your heat to low, and stir regularly as you complete the following steps.

3. Bring a pot of water to a simmer and add 1 teaspoon vinegar. Break your eggs into a bowl. Stir the water, and gently transfer your eggs to the water. Cook for 3 min. Remove the eggs from the water and transfer them onto a kitchen towel. Season with salt and black pepper.

4. Remove your potato hash from the heat and add red onions, feta, and parsley. Gently nestle your poached eggs in your hash.

5. Cover the hash in sealed containers and refrigerate for 3-5 days.

6. Serve with pickled cucumbers and poached eggs.

ITALY BREAKFAST BOWL

Serves: 6

Prep Time: 10 min.

Cook Time: 20 min.

INGREDIENTS:

12 medium eggs

¼ cup (60 ml) plain Greek yogurt

1 tsp. onion powder

1 tsp. garlic powder

½ tsp. salt

½ tsp. black pepper

1 tsp. extra virgin olive oil

5 oz. (140 g) baby spinach

2½ cups (450 g) cherry tomatoes, halved

1 avocado, sliced

2 cups (370 g) quinoa, cooked

DIRECTIONS:

1. Add eggs, yogurt, onion powder, garlic powder, salt, and black pepper to a large bowl. Whisk everything together.

2. Heat extra virgin olive oil in a large skillet. Add your spinach and cook for 3–4 min., until the spinach is just wilted.

3. Add halved cherry tomatoes. Cook for 3–4 minutes until they have softened.

4. Add the egg mixture. Cook for 7–9 min., constantly stirring, until the eggs have set and are scrambled.

5. Add quinoa. Cook for a few min. to warm.

6. Cool, cover in sealed containers, and refrigerate for 3-5 days.

7. Serve with sliced avocado and poached egg. Sprinkle with lemon juice.

NUTRITION FACTS (PER SERVING):

Calories: 357, Carbohydrates: 20 g, Protein: 23 g, Fat: 20 g, Fiber: 3 g, Sugar: 4 g

VEGETABLE HASH

Serves: 3

Prep Time: 10 min.

Cook Time: 40 min.

NUTRITION FACTS (PER SERVING):

Calories: 391, Carbohydrates: 73 g, Protein: 10.8 g, Fat: 7.1 g, Fiber: 14.4 g, Sugar: 17.4 g

INGREDIENTS:

2 bell peppers (230 g), diced

1 can (15 oz./425 g) chickpeas, drained and rinsed

1 tsp. garlic powder

1-2 Tbsp. extra virgin olive oil

½ large (50 g) onion, chopped

1½ lb. (700 g) sweet potatoes, cubed

1 lb. (450 g) broccoli florets

2 medium carrots (120 g), cubed

salt and black pepper to taste

Sauce:

½ lemon, juiced

pinch of salt

sriracha

4 Tbsp. tahini

4 Tbsp. water

DIRECTIONS:

1. Set your oven to 425°F (218°C) and grease your sheet pan well.

2. Mix the vegetables and chickpeas with the oil and spices, then arrange them in a single layer on the sheet pan. Roast on the center rack for 20 minutes and toss halfway through.

3. Higher your oven to 500°F (260°C) and stir the mixture a second time. Allow to bake for a further 20 min., again stirring halfway through. Set aside to cool.

4. While roasting the vegetables, prepare the dressing by combining the ingredients in a small bowl. For ultimate flavor, allow the dressing to rest.

5. Toss the vegetables with the dressing and serve with sliced radish.

6. Keep the dish in the refrigerator for 4-5 days or in the freezer for 2-3 months.

ITALIAN SPINACH FRITTATA

Serves: 8

Prep Time: 15 min.

Cook Time: 1 hour

NUTRITION FACTS (PER SERVING):

Calories: 366, Carbohydrates: 23.9 g, Protein: 28.2 g, Fat: 14.5 g, Fiber: 5.7 g, Sugar: 6.7 g

INGREDIENTS:

2 Tbsp. extra virgin olive oil

1 lb. (450 g) Italian turkey / chicken sausage, skinless

1 yellow onion (70 g), chopped

½ tsp. salt

5 oz. (140 g) fresh spinach, chopped

8 medium eggs

1 cup (250 ml) plain milk

6 slices whole-grain bread, cut into bite-sized pieces

1 cup (116 g) sun-dried tomatoes, sliced

1 can (14 oz./400 g) artichoke hearts, drained

½ cup (60 g) feta cheese, crumbled

DIRECTIONS:

1. Heat 1 tablespoon olive oil in a large skillet over medium-high heat. Add your sausages and cook for 8 min., breaking it up as you cook. Transfer the sausages to a paper towel.

2. Add another tablespoon of olive oil to your skillet. Add chopped onion and salt. Cook for 5 min. Add chopped spinach and cook for 1 minute.

3. Beat eggs in a bowl and add milk. Add bread bites, sliced sun-dried tomatoes, artichokes, feta, and sausage mixture.

4. Spray a baking dish with cooking spray.

5. Pour the mixture into a baking dish, cover, and refrigerate for at least 1 hour and up to overnight.

6. Preheat your oven to 350°F (177°C). Take out your casserole and let it sit for 30 min.

7. Bake for 45 min. Remove from the oven, and let it sit for 10 minutes before serving.

8. Keep the frittata in the refrigerator for 4-5 days.

OAT GRANOLA WITH BERRIES

Serves: 6

Prep Time: 5 min.

Cook Time: 5 min.

INGREDIENTS:

½ cup (40 g) oats

⅓ cup (40 g) pumpkin seeds

2 Tbsp. sunflower seeds

1 Tbsp. flax seeds

2 Tbsp. shredded coconut

2 Tbsp. honey

1 tsp. cinnamon

1 tsp. coconut oil, softened

yogurt or milk

fresh berries (for serving)

DIRECTIONS:

1. Mix together all of the ingredients in a bowl.

2. Heat a nonstick pan over medium heat, and add your mixture. Cook for 3–5 min. to toast, stirring frequently.

3. Remove from heat and let your granola cool. Store in sealed containers for 2 weeks.

4. Serve with berries and yogurt or milk.

NUTRITION FACTS (PER SERVING):

Calories: 120, Carbohydrates: 14 g, Protein: 3 g, Fat: 7 g, Fiber: 2 g, Sugar: 7 g

OVERNIGHT OATS WITH PEANUT BUTTER

Serves: 1

Prep Time: 10 min.

Total Time: 8 hours

INGREDIENTS:

½ cup (40 g) old-fashioned rolled oats

1/6 tsp. salt

2 Tbsp. fresh raspberries

1 Tbsp. toasted pine nuts

1 Tbsp. raspberry jam

¼ tsp. cinnamon

2 Tbsp. peanut butter

1 Tbsp. coconut flakes

DIRECTIONS:

1. Mix oats, salt, and ½ cup of water in a bowl. Cover and refrigerate overnight.

2. Heat the oats or serve cold. Top with the rest of your ingredients.

NUTRITION FACTS (PER SERVING):

Calories: 282, Carbohydrates: 48.2 g, Protein: 6.7 g, Fat: 8.9 g, Fiber: 6.1 g, Sugar: 18.7 g

GREEK GYRO

Servings: 8

Prep Time + Cook Time: 2 hours

NUTRITION FACTS (PER SERVING)

Calories 459; Total Fat 14.7 g, Saturated Fat 6.5 g, Cholesterol 75 mg, Sodium 412 mg, Total Carbohydrates 55.8 g, Dietary Fiber 10.6 g, Total Sugars 6.3 g, Protein 30.2 g, Vitamin D 0 mcg, Calcium 171 mg, Iron 4 mg, Potassium 746 mg

INGREDIENTS:

For dough:

1¼ cup (300 ml) lukewarm water

2 Tbsp. olive oil

3½ cups (500 g, 15¾ oz.) whole grain flour

¼ tsp. sea salt

1 package active dry yeast

After beeping:

1 tsp. dried oregano

For filling:

1.1 pounds (500 g) pork fillet

2 onions (140 g), sliced

½ cup (60 g) fresh chili pepper, finely chopped

1⅔ cup (200 g) Feta cheese

8 cherry tomatoes (140 g)

For fill:

1½ (360 ml) sour cream

Pepper, salt

DIRECTIONS:

1. Knead the dough in a bread machine or by hand. Let it rest for 45 minutes.

2. Cut the pork into small thin slices and slightly roast it in a frying pan. Be careful not to overcook it.

3. Take the dough out of the bread maker, roll it out evenly, and place it (forming a board) on a baking sheet covered with oiled parchment paper.

4. Season the dairy cream with salt and pepper, and evenly spread it over the dough. Cover with roast pork, onion rings, tomatoes, and chili peppers. Sprinkle with diced feta cheese.

5. Leave in a warm place for 30 minutes to rest and rise.

6. Preheat the oven to 400°F (205°C).

7. Bake for 25-30 minutes (until golden brown).

GREEK HUMMUS TOAST

Serves: 4

Prep Time: 10 min.

Total Time: 10 min.

INGREDIENTS:

4 slices whole-grain bread

½ cup (120 g) hummus

za'atar spice blend

a handful of arugula

1 cup (200 g) baked pumpkin, sliced/chopped

1-2 Roma tomatoes (150 – 250 g), chopped

2 Tbsp. olives, chopped

feta cheese, crumbled

1 tsp. sesame seeds, for sprinkling

DIRECTIONS:

1. Toast your bread.

2. Spread 2 tablespoons of hummus on each slice of bread. Add a pinch or two of za'atar on top of each slice.

3. Load on the rest of your ingredients, and serve.

NUTRITION FACTS (PER SERVING):

Calories: 166, Carbohydrates: 29.4 g, Protein: 6.1 g, Fat: 4.2 g, Sugar: 4.7 g

SMOOTHIE BOWL WITH GRANOLA

Serves: 1

Prep Time: 10 min.

Total Time: 10 min.

INGREDIENTS:

⅔ cup (100 g) frozen raspberries

½ cup (75 g) frozen bananas, sliced

½ cup (120 ml) unsweetened almond milk

5 Tbsp. roasted almonds

¼ tsp. cinnamon

⅛ tsp. cardamom

⅛ tsp. vanilla extract

¼ cup (40 g) fresh blueberries

1 Tbsp. unsweetened coconut flakes

DIRECTIONS:

1. Blend your raspberries, banana, almond milk, 3 tablespoons of almonds, cinnamon, vanilla, and cardamom until smooth.

2. Pour your smoothie into a bowl and sprinkle with coconut, the rest of your almonds, and blueberries.

NUTRITION FACTS (PER SERVING):

Calories: 360, Carbohydrates: 45.6 g, Protein: 9.2 g, Fat: 19 g, Fiber: 14 g, Sugar: 21.4 g

MINI EGG QUICHES

Serves: 6

Prep Time: 20 min.

Cook Time: 25 min.

NUTRITION FACTS (PER SERVING):

Calories: 266, Carbohydrates: 18.2 g, Protein: 12.4 g, Fat: 16.2 g, Fiber: 2.1 g, Sugar: 2.4 g

INGREDIENTS:

3 Tbsp. extra virgin olive oil

⅓ cup (70 g) red onion, diced

¼ tsp. salt

6 medium eggs

10 oz. (285 g) frozen chopped spinach, thawed and squeezed dry

½ cup (60 g) feta cheese, crumbled

½ cup (120 ml) plain milk

¼ cup (10 g) dill, chopped

½ tsp. black pepper

8 sheets thawed phyllo (9x14 inches/22.5x35 cm)/shortcrust pastry for mini quiches

DIRECTIONS:

1. Preheat your oven to 350°F (177°C). Spray a 12-cup muffin tin with cooking spray.

2. Heat 1 tablespoon olive oil in a skillet over medium heat. Add your onion and half of your salt. Cook, often stirring, for 4 min. Remove from heat.

3. Whisk together eggs, spinach, milk, feta cheese, pepper, dill, the rest of your salt, and cooked onions in a large bowl.

4. Lay out phyllo sheets, and cover them with a clean kitchen towel (to keep them from drying out).

5. Add 2 tablespoons olive oil to a small bowl. Brush one sheet of phyllo with oil, and cut it into 6 pieces. Place one square in a muffin cup, and press it down gently. Place another square on top so that the edges overlap. Repeat for the rest of your phyllo.

6. Fill each cup with ¼ cup of the egg mixture.

7. Bake for 25–30 min.

8. Store in the fridge for 3-5 days. Eat warm.

SNACKS

APPETIZING WRAPS

Serves: 4

Prep Time: 15 min.

Cook Time: 15 min.

NUTRITION FACTS (PER SERVING):

Calories: 567, Carbohydrates: 55 g, Protein: 31 g, Fat: 25 g, Fiber: 7 g, Sugar: 7 g

INGREDIENTS:

6 garlic cloves, minced

12 oz. (340 g) salmon filets

1½ tsp. dried basil

½ tsp. black pepper

salt

2 chopped cucumbers, plus ½ minced cucumber

⅓ cup (60 g) olives

2 Tbsp. pickled jalapeño slices (optional)

4 Tbsp. chopped parsley

1 avocado (150 g), chopped

lettuce leaves

½ lemon, juiced

1 tsp. extra virgin olive oil

1 cup (240 ml) Greek yogurt

4 tortillas or flatbread (for serving)

DIRECTIONS:

1. Rub the salmon with basil, 2 minced garlic cloves, and pepper. Cook in a pan for 5–6 minutes per side, or until golden brown all over. Transfer to a plate and break up the salmon into bite-sized pieces.

2. Mix Greek yogurt, minced cucumber, a pinch of salt, and 3 of your minced garlic cloves in a small bowl.

3. Add chopped cucumbers, avocado, arugula, parsley, lemon juice, jalapeño (if using), olives, olive oil, a pinch of salt, and 1 minced garlic clove to another bowl. Mix to combine.

4. Fill a tortilla or flatbread with some tzatziki, salad, and salmon. Wrap and serve.

BEEF WRAPS

Serves: 4

Prep Time: 15 min.

Cook Time: 15 min.

INGREDIENTS:

1 lb. (450 g) beef fillet, chopped and cooked

½ cup (120 ml) Greek yogurt

½ cup jarred roasted red peppers, patted dry and chopped

4 cherry tomatoes (80 g), diced

1 red onion (70 g), diced

½ cup (90 g) Kalamata olives, chopped

1 tsp lemon zest

2 tsp lemon juice

½ tsp. salt

¼ tsp. black pepper

4 whole-wheat tortillas

4 lettuce leaves

DIRECTIONS:

1. Mix cooked beef pieces, red peppers, olives, yogurt, lemon juice and zest, salt, and black pepper in a large bowl.

2. In each tortilla, arrange lettuce leaves, beef mixture, cucumber, and tomato slices. Roll tightly, slice in half, and serve.

NUTRITION FACTS (PER SERVING):

Calories: 449, Carbohydrates: 20 g, Protein: 45 g, Fat: 20 g, Fiber: 2 g, Sugar: 4 g

PITA STUFFED WITH CHICKEN

Serves: 1

Prep Time: 10 min.

Cook Time: 10 min.

INGREDIENTS:

1 tbsp. lemon juice

1 chicken breast (180 g), boneless, skinless

salt

black pepper

1 whole-grain pita

2 lettuce leaves

5–6 cucumber slices

1 Roma tomato (150 g), diced

1 small red onion (50 g), diced

1 Tbsp. fresh parsley, chopped

1 Tbsp. tahini

DIRECTIONS:

1. Squeeze lemon juice all over a chicken breast and rub in a pinch or two of salt and pepper.

2. Place the chicken breast on a grill or grill pan and cook over medium-high heat for 10–15 min.

3. Remove from heat, and let it cool for about 5 minutes before cutting your chicken breast into strips.

4. Cut your pita in half, making two pockets.

5. Fill each pocket with lettuce, chicken, cucumber, tomato, onion, and parsley.

6. Drizzle with tahini.

NUTRITION FACTS (PER SERVING):

Calories: 320, Carbohydrates: 38 g, Protein: 34 g, Fat: 4.5 g, Fiber: 5 g, Sugar: 5 g

SALMON SPINACH WRAPS

Serves: 3

Prep Time: 15 min.

Cook Time: 5 min.

INGREDIENTS:

1 smoked salmon fillet (180 g), sliced

1 can (12 oz./340 g) corn kernels, rinsed and drained

2 garlic cloves, minced

½ tsp. dried mint

1 ½ Tbsp. tahini

1 Tbsp. lemon juice

1 tsp. red pepper flakes

½ cup (15 g) spinach

hummus

½ cup diced tomato, cucumber, avocado salad

4 tortillas or pita wraps

DIRECTIONS:

1. Combine corn kernels, 1 minced garlic clove, dried mint, and red pepper flakes.

2. Mix tahini, lemon juice, and remaining garlic. Add 1–2 tablespoons of water until your sauce reaches your desired level of creaminess.

3. To assemble the wraps, add some spinach, salmon slices, 2–3 tablespoons of the corn mixture, 2 tablespoons of hummus, and 2–3 tablespoons of tomato-cucumber salad to a tortilla. Spread 1 tablespoon of sauce over everything, and wrap the tortilla up tightly.

4. Store your ingredients separately for meal prepping.

NUTRITION FACTS (PER SERVING):

Calories: 485, Carbohydrates: 66 g, Protein: 16 g, Fat: 19 g, Fiber: 11 g, Sugar: 7 g

ITALIAN SANDWICH WITH GRILLED FETA CHEESE

Serves: 1

Prep Time: 5 min.

Cook Time: 5 min.

INGREDIENTS:

2 slices whole-wheat sandwich bread

1 tsp salted butter

2 slices feta cheese

¼ cup (20 g) kale

3 red onion slices

1 slice tomato

2 Tbsp. black olives

DIRECTIONS:

1. Heat a skillet. Butter 1 side of both slices of bread and place them butter-side down on the skillet.

2. Add kale, cheese, onions, tomato, and olives to one slice of bread, and place the other slice of bread on top of everything.

3. Grill on both sides until the cheese has melted.

NUTRITION FACTS (PER SERVING):

Calories: 438, Carbohydrates: 31.6 g, Protein: 20 g, Fat: 26.2 g, Fiber: 7 g, Sugar: 7 g

ITALIAN MARGHERITA

Serves: 8

Prep Time: 10 min.

Cook Time: 18 min.

INGREDIENTS:

whole-wheat pizza crust

2 Tbsp. extra virgin olive oil

½ cup (120 ml) canned tomatoes, crushed or diced

½ cup (60 g) mozzarella, shredded

12 fresh basil leaves

3—4 Roma tomatoes (450 – 600 g), sliced

DIRECTIONS:

1. Preheat the oven to 425°F (218°C). Place a pizza stone in the middle of your oven rack.

2. Place a large sheet of parchment paper on your counter. Roll out your pizza crust to your desired thickness.

3. Spread about 1 tablespoon of olive oil over the crust.

4. Spread canned tomatoes on the crust so they reach ½ inch away from the crust's edge.

5. Sprinkle with cheese.

6. Top the pizza off with the rest of the ingredients.

7. Bake for 15–18 minutes, or until the crust begins to brown and everything appears done. Remove from the oven, slice into 8 slices, and serve.

NUTRITION FACTS (PER SERVING):

Calories: 250, Carbohydrates: 30 g, Fat: 12.8 g, Fiber: 3 g

NEAPOLITAN PIZZA

Serves: 8

Prep Time: 10 min.

Cook Time: 30 min.

INGREDIENTS:

1 batch pizza dough

1 Tbsp. extra virgin olive oil

2 tsp. garlic, minced

1½ cups (170 g) mozzarella, shredded

4 oz. (113 g) smoked chicken breast, sliced

2 cups (60 g) spinach

6–8 grape tomatoes (850 g), sliced

½ red onion (35 g), sliced

½ cup (60 g) feta cheese, crumbled

chopped parsley, optional

DIRECTIONS:

1. Preheat the oven to 400°F (205°C).

2. Bake your pizza dough for 8 min. Remove from the oven and drizzle with olive oil.

3. Add garlic, mozzarella, spinach, tomatoes, sliced chicken, red onion, and feta. Sprinkle with parsley.

4. Bake for 15–20 min.

5. Let it cool for 5–10 minutes before slicing and serving.

NUTRITION FACTS (PER SERVING):

Calories: 296, Carbohydrates: 30 g, Protein: 11 g, Fat: 15 g, Fiber: 4 g, Sugar: 3 g

SOUPS & STEWS

FRENCH SHRIMP SOUP

Serves: 6

Prep Time: 10 min.

Cook Time: 25 min.

NUTRITION FACTS (PER SERVING):

Calories: 307, Carbohydrates: 32 g, Protein: 27.4 g, Fat: 10.4 g, Sugar: 7 g

8 oz. (230 g) scallops

salt

black pepper

extra virgin olive oil

1½ lb. (675 g) shrimp, peeled and deveined

1 medium green bell pepper (120 g), chopped

1 medium red bell pepper (120 g), chopped

1 yellow onion (70 g), chopped

6 garlic cloves, minced

3 Tbsp. tomato paste

1 Tbsp. dried oregano

7 cups (1.7 L) chicken (vegetable) broth

1 small zucchini (250 g), diced

1 cup (112 g) whole-wheat orzo

1 cup (60 g) fresh parsley, chopped

1 cup (20 g) fresh dill, chopped

1 lemon, juiced

red pepper flakes (optional)

crusty whole-wheat bread

DIRECTIONS:

1. Pat scallops dry and season with salt and pepper.

2. Heat 1 tablespoon of olive oil in a skillet over medium-high heat. Add scallops, and sear for 1½ minutes per side until golden-brown. Sprinkle with oregano, and transfer them to a plate.

3. Add 1 tablespoon of olive oil, and add shrimp. Sear for 2 minutes per side. Remove from the heat, and sprinkle with oregano.

4. Heat 1 tablespoon of olive oil in a pot. Add bell peppers, onion, garlic, tomato paste, oregano, and salt. Cook for 5 minutes.

5. Pour in broth and bring it to a boil. Add diced zucchini, and cook for 3–5 min.

6. Once boiling, add orzo. Cook for 8 min. Add chopped dill, lemon juice, and parsley. Add scallops and shrimp, stirring for 1–2 min. Remove from heat.

7. Season to taste. Add red pepper flakes, and serve with crusty bread.

8. Keep in a fridge for 3-5 days.

GREEK LENTIL VEGETABLE SOUP

Serves: 6

Prep Time: 20 min.

Cook Time: 20 min.

INGREDIENTS:

1 bay leaf

1 cup (200 g) uncooked brown lentils

2 carrots (120 g), finely chopped

2 celery ribs (100 g), finely chopped

4 garlic cloves, minced

1 small lemon, juiced

3 Tbsp. extra virgin olive oil

1 onion (70 g), diced

2 sprigs fresh rosemary

1 tsp. sea salt

6 sprigs fresh thyme

2 Tbsp. tomato paste

40 oz. (1.1 L) vegetable stock

DIRECTIONS:

1. Over medium heat, heat the oil and add the onion. Cook for 7 minutes, until gloriously browning and translucent. Stir in the garlic and heat for 1 minute.

2. Add the tomato paste to the mix and cook for another 2-3 min.

3. Mix in the rest of the ingredients (except the lemon juice), cover, and bring to a boil. Reduce the heat and simmer for 35-40 min. The lentils should be as soft as you like.

4. Take the herbs out and purée as much as you want. The more you purée, the thicker it will be. Stir in the lemon juice and eat up!

5. Place in airtight containers for up to 4 days in the fridge and 6 months in the freezer.

NUTRITIONAL FACTS (PER SERVING):

Calories: 211, Carbohydrates: 28 g, Protein: 9 g, Fat: 8 g, Sugar: 5 g

CHICKEN CAULIFLOWER SOUP

Serves: 4

Prep Time: 10 min.

Cook Time: 40 min.

INGREDIENTS:

1 lb. (450 g) bone-in chicken thighs

1 medium potato (170 g), peeled and chopped

1 medium carrot (60 g), chopped

1 white onion (70 g), chopped

2 Tbsp. dried mint

1 Tbsp. turmeric

1 Tbsp. ginger, grated

½ cup (50 g) cauliflower florets, chopped

DIRECTIONS:

1. Cook chicken with 4–5 cups of water in a small pot. Once the water begins boiling, add chopped onion, potato, turmeric, and mint. Cover with a lid, and let it cook over medium-high heat for 20–30 min.

2. Transfer the chicken to a bowl with cool water, and let it sit for a few minutes to cool down.

3. Take the meat off the bone, and shred the chicken using two forks.

4. Add the chicken and water from the bowl into the pot. Add chopped carrot, ginger, cauliflower, and salt and pepper to taste. Cook for 5–10 minutes.

5. Keep in a fridge for 5-6 days. Serve warm.

NUTRITION FACTS (PER SERVING):

Calories: 305, Carbohydrates: 14 g, Protein: 29 g, Fat: 16 g, Fiber: 2 g, Sugar: 2 g

ITALIAN MINESTRONE

Serves: 6 - 8

Prep Time: 15 min.

Cook Time: 1¼ hours

NUTRITION FACTS (PER SERVING):

Calories: 879, Total Fat: 20 g, Saturated Fat: 5 g, Cholesterol: 110 mg, Sodium: 2030 mg, Total Carbohydrate: 132 g, Dietary Fiber: 18 g, Total Sugar: 10 g, Protein: 41 g, Vitamin D: 1 mcg, Calcium: 321 mg, Iron: 12 mg, Potassium: 1708 mg

2 Tbsp. olive oil

1½ cups (350 g) yellow onions, chopped

4 oz. (115 g) pancetta, diced into ½-inch portions

2 cups carrots (240 g), diced to ½-inch sizes

2 cups celery (200 g), diced to ½-inch sizes

2½ cups (500 g) butternut squash, peeled, diced

2 tsp. fresh thyme leaves, chopped

1½ Tbsp. garlic, minced

1 can (26 oz./740 g) tomatoes, diced

6-8 cups (1½ – 2 L) chicken stock

1 bay leaf

Salt and black pepper to taste

1 can (15 oz./425 g) cannellini beans, drained and rinsed

2 cups (400 g) cooked pasta (small-sized)

½ cup (120 ml) dry white wine

Garlic bruschetta/whole-grain Italian bread/breadsticks

parmesan cheese, shredded

9- 10 oz. (255 – 285 g) fresh baby spinach leaves

DIRECTIONS:

1. Place your Dutch oven over medium heat and add 2 Tbsp. of olive oil. Add pancetta and cook for about 6-8 minutes.

2. Add chopped onion, celery, carrot, squash, garlic, and thyme and cook for 8-10 minutes over medium heat, making sure to keep stirring it from time to time.

3. Once the veggies are tender, add 6 cups of chicken stock, 1 tablespoon of salt, bay leaf, and 1½ teaspoon of pepper to your pot.

4. Bring the mix to a boil and lower the heat. Simmer (uncovered) for 30 minutes. Discard bay leaf.

5. Add beans and cooked pasta, and heat it thoroughly. Add more chicken stock. Add spinach and toss the soup with a large spoon. Stir in white wine and pesto and season with salt to taste.

6. Store in a fridge for 3-5 days.

7. Serve with bruschetta on top. Sprinkle with cheese and drizzle with olive oil.

SICILIAN FISH STEW

Serves: 4 - 5

Prep Time: 10 min.

Cook Time: 35 min.

NUTRITION FACTS (PER SERVING):

Calories: 395, Total Fat: 11 g, Saturated Fat: 2 g, Cholesterol: 63 mg, Sodium: 144 mg, Total Carbohydrate: 34 g, Dietary Fiber: 5 g, Total Sugar: 6 g, Protein: 31 g, Vitamin D: 0 mcg, Calcium: 91 mg, Iron: 2mg, Potassium: 899 mg

1 large yellow onion (90 g), chopped

2 celery ribs (100 g), chopped

Salt and black pepper to taste

4 large garlic cloves, minced

Extra virgin olive oil

½ tsp. thyme, dried

¾ cup (180 ml) dry white wine

1 can (28 oz./800 g) whole peeled plum tomatoes, juiced, separated, and reserved

3 cups (720 ml) vegetable stock

2 Tbsp. capers

¼ cup (35 g) golden raisins

2 lb. (900 g) sea bass fillet, 1½-inch thick, cut into large cubes (skinless)

½ cup (30 g) fresh parsley, chopped

Crusty Italian bread /pita bread for serving

3 Tbsp. toasted pine nuts for serving

DIRECTIONS:

1. Add 1 tablespoon of olive oil to a Dutch oven and let it heat up.

2. Add chopped onion, salt, black pepper, and celery and cook for about 4 minutes until tender. Add red pepper flakes, thyme, and garlic and cook for 30 seconds until a nice fragrant comes.

3. Stir in white wine and your reserved tomato juice (from a can).

4. Lower heat and bring the mix to a simmer. Keep cooking until it is reduced by half.

5. Add tomatoes, raisins, vegetable stock, and capers and cook for 15-20 minutes over medium heat until the flavors mix well.

6. Pat fish dry and season it gently with pepper and salt.

7. Transfer the fish pieces into the stew and gently stir until the fish is covered well. Bring the mix to a simmer and cook for 5 minutes.

8. Remove the Dutch oven from your heat and cover it. Let it sit for about 4-5 minutes to allow flavors to sip into the fish.

9. Once the fish is flaky, stir in chopped-up parsley.

10. Keep in a fridge for 3-5 days.

11. Ladle the stew into serving bowls and top with toasted pine nuts. Serve and enjoy with crusty Italian bread.

ITALIAN SEAFOOD STEW

Serves: 6

Prep Time: 45 min.

Cook Time: 1¼ hours

NUTRITION FACTS (PER SERVING):

Calories: 626, Total Fat: 25 g, Saturated Fat: 4 g, Cholesterol: 144 mg, Sodium: 2187 mg, Total Carbohydrate: 38 g, Dietary Fiber: 8 g, Total Sugar: 14 g, Protein: 65 g, Vitamin D: 1 mcg, Calcium: 201 mg, Iron: 15 mg, Potassium: 2623 mg

1/2 cup (120 ml) extra virgin olive oil

2 celery ribs (100 g), finely chopped

1 fennel bulb, cored and chopped

1 white onion (70 g), finely chopped

1 Tbsp. dried oregano

Pinch of ground red pepper

1½ lb. (675 g) squids, cleaned, bodies cut into ½-inch rings, tentacles halved

2 cups (480 ml) dry white wine

1 can (28 oz./800 g) tomato puree

2 cups (480 ml) water

 Salt and black pepper to taste

2 lemons, zest of one peeled in strips, zest of other grated

1 cup (240 ml) bottled clam broth

12 oz. (340 g) mussels, scrubbed

12-oz. (340 g) littleneck clams, scrubbed

12 oz. (340 g) skinless striped bass fillet, cut into 2 by 1-inch pieces

12 oz. (340 g) shrimp, shelled and deveined

2 Tbsp. flat-leaf parsley, chopped

DIRECTIONS:

1. Add ½ cup (120 ml) of olive oil to your Dutch oven and heat it up.

2. Add celery, fennel, onion, oregano, and crushed red pepper and cook for 15 minutes. Add squid and cook over low heat for 15 minutes. Stir in wine and bring to a boil over high heat. Cook for 20 minutes.

3. Stir in the tomato puree and lemon zest strips. Season with salt and pepper. Cook on low-high heat for 40 minutes until thick.

4. Add water and clam broth, and bring to a boil. Remove and discard the lemon zest. Season broth with salt and pepper.

5. Add mussels, shrimp, clams, and cover. Cook for 5 minutes until most shells are open. Add striped bass and cook for 2 minutes.

6. Take a small bowl, add parsley, and grated lemon zest.

7. Store in a fridge for 3-5 days.

8. Drizzle with oil and serve with rice/pasta/whole-grain bread!

APPETIZING SOUP WITH RED LENTILS

Serves: 3

Prep Time: 10 min.

Cook Time: 25 min.

INGREDIENTS:

2 cups (60 g) fresh spinach

2 medium onions (140 g), chopped

⅓ cup (60 g) dry, coarse bulgur

½ cup (100 g) red lentils, soaked

1 medium potato (170 g), chopped

½ red pepper, finely chopped

½ tsp. turmeric powder

1 Tbsp. ground ginger

½ tsp. cumin

1 Tbsp. paprika

1 garlic clove, minced

black pepper

fresh mint leaves, chopped

2 Tbsp. extra virgin olive oil

sea salt

DIRECTIONS:

1. Rinse and drain lentils and bulgur.

2. Heat 1 tablespoon of olive oil in a cooking pot. Add minced garlic and chopped onion, and cook over medium-high heat for 1 minute.

3. Add spices and a few tablespoons of water. Add lentils, bulgur, spinach, red pepper, mint, 2½ cups of water, and potatoes or beets. The water should be covering everything. Cover with a lid and cook for 25–30 min. Check on it periodically, and add more water when needed.

4. Turn off the heat, and add 1 tablespoon of olive oil.

5. Store in a fridge for 4-5 days. Serve warm.

NUTRITION FACTS (PER SERVING):

Calories: 290, Carbohydrates: 43 g, Protein: 12 g, Fat: 11 g, Fiber: 12g, Sugar: 9 g

MAIN DISHES

CHICKPEA STEW

Serves: 2 | Prep Time: 8 min. | Cook Time: 7 min.

INGREDIENTS:

1 can (15 oz./425 g)
chickpeas, rinsed and drained

4 tomatoes (480 g), chopped

1 zucchini (320 g), chopped

1 white onion (70 g), chopped

1 bell pepper (120 g), sliced

1 tsp chili powder

2 minced garlic cloves

1 Tbsp. extra virgin olive oil

1 Tbsp. sesame seeds

1 tsp. nigella seeds (optional)

10 basil leaves, chopped

DIRECTIONS:

1. Add chopped tomatoes and onion to a large pan, cover with a lid, and cook over medium-high heat for 3–4 min.

2. Add chickpeas and stir. Put the lid back on, and let it simmer for 5 min.

3. Add garlic, chopped zucchini, and sliced bell pepper. Stir, cover, and cook for 2 min.

4. Turn off the heat, add basil leaves and olive oil, and sprinkle with seeds and chili powder on top.

5. Store in a fridge for 4-5 days. Serve warm with your favorite sides (pasta, rice, mashed vegetables, etc.).

NUTRITION FACTS (PER SERVING):

Calories: 446, Carbohydrates: 66 g, Protein: 20 g, Fat: 14 g, Fiber: 18 g, Sugar: 19 g

BAKED SALMON

Serves: 4

Prep time: 10 min.

Cook time: 15 min.

INGREDIENTS:

4 (4-oz./113 g) salmon fillets

Salt and pepper to taste

1 cup (120 g) whole grain breadcrumbs

2 Tbsp. chives, chopped

½ tsp. garlic powder

½ tsp. onion powder

2 Tbsp. parsley, chopped

1 tsp. lemon peel, grated

¼ cup (60 ml) lemon juice

DIRECTIONS:

1. Preheat your oven to 400°F (205°C), and line it carefully with baking paper.
2. Season the salmon on both sides with salt and pepper.
3. Place the seasoned salmon on the casserole baking dish.
4. Mix the breadcrumbs, chives, garlic powder, onion powder, parsley, and lemon peel in a blender or food processor.
5. Top the salmon with the lemon juice and processed mixture.
6. Drizzle the coated salmon with canola oil.
7. Cook for 12-15 minutes.
8. Enjoy the warm salmon with your favorite salad, curry, or sauce.
9. Keep in a fridge for 3-4 days.

NUTRITION FACTS (PER SERVING):

Calories 264, Total Fat 8.6 g, Saturated Fat 1.4 g, Cholesterol 50 mg, Sodium 399 mg, Total Carbohydrates 20.6 g, Dietary Fiber 1.5 g, Total Sugars 2.3 g, Protein 25.9 g, Calcium 97 mg, Iron 2 mg, Potassium 532 mg

MEDITERRANEAN GROUND BEEF WITH VEGETABLES

Serves: 5

Prep Time: 10 min.

Cook Time: 12 min.

INGREDIENTS:

16 oz. (450 g) ground beef

1 small zucchini (250 g), diced

1 bell pepper (120 g), diced

4 cherry tomatoes (70 g), sliced

½ cup (70 g) sweet potato, diced

1 yellow onion (70 g), thinly sliced

2 garlic cloves, minced

10 Kalamata olives (40 g), sliced

1 Tbsp. coriander

1 Tbsp. fresh rosemary, chopped

1 Tbsp. fresh oregano, chopped

1 Tbsp. paprika

DIRECTIONS:

1. Heat a cast-iron skillet over medium heat.

2. Add diced zucchini, bell pepper, sweet potato, garlic, onion, and sauté for 5 min., stirring often.

3. Add ground beef, and cook for 10 - 15 min. until lightly browned.

4. Add coriander and tomatoes, and cook for 5 minutes over medium-high heat.

5. Remove from heat, and stir in sliced olives and herbs.

6. Store in a fridge for 4-5 days. Serve warm with rice/pasta/mashed potato.

NUTRITION FACTS (PER SERVING):

Calories: 360, Carbohydrates: 28 g, Protein: 22 g, Fat: 18 g, Sugar: 5 g

COUSCOUS WITH TURKEY

Serves: 2

Prep Time: 7 min.

Cook Time: 13 min.

INGREDIENTS:

6 oz. (170 g) turkey fillet, chopped

2 cups (360 g) couscous, cooked

1 medium carrot (60 g), chopped

½ red bell pepper (55 g), chopped

½ tsp. turmeric powder

2 tsp. paprika

1 tsp. cumin

1 Tbsp. pickled jalapeños

½ tsp. black pepper

1 tsp. red pepper flakes

½ tsp. coriander

2 Tbsp. extra virgin olive oil

4 minced garlic cloves

salt

1 Tbsp. parsley, chopped

DIRECTIONS:

1. Cook turkey pieces in a pan with ⅓ cup of water over medium-high heat. Cover and cook for 4–5 min.

2. Add turmeric, black pepper, red pepper flakes, cumin, coriander, 1 teaspoon paprika, and 1 garlic clove. Stir for 2–3 minutes, or until all the water has evaporated.

3. Reduce heat to medium and stir in cooked couscous, carrot, bell pepper, 1 tablespoon of olive oil, the rest of the paprika, and a pinch of salt. Cook for 3–4 min.

4. Stir in the rest of the garlic, jalapeño, and 1 tablespoon of olive oil. Stir for 2 min. and remove from heat.

5. Store in a fridge in meal prep containers for 3-5 days. Serve with chopped parsley.

NUTRITION FACTS (PER SERVING):

Calories: 443, Carbohydrates: 18 g, Protein: 28 g, Fat: 31 g, Fiber: 7 g, Sugar: 6 g

PASTA WITH GROUND BEEF

Serves: 4

Prep Time: 20 min.

Cook Time: 15 min.

NUTRITION FACTS (PER SERVING):

Calories: 472, Carbohydrates: 35.7 g, Protein: 34.4 g, Fat: 20.3 g,
Fiber: 4.3 g, Sugar: 3.9 g

1 lb. (450 g) ground beef

1 tbsp. plus ¼ tsp. dried dill

salt

black pepper

5.3 oz. (150 g) Greek yogurt

1 red onion (70 g), sliced

white wine vinegar

2 garlic cloves, minced

1 Tbsp. extra virgin olive oil

1½ tsp. dried oregano

½ cucumber, chopped

½ cucumber, sliced

2 cups pasta (400 g), cooked

hummus

4 Tbsp. Parmesan cheese, shredded

pita wedges

Sriracha

DIRECTIONS:

1. Mix yogurt, chopped cucumber, olive oil, garlic, ¼ tsp dried dill and a pinch or two of salt and pepper in a food processor. Pulse until everything is combined. Stick it in the fridge until you are ready to serve.

2. Place red onion slices in a shallow bowl and pour white wine vinegar over it so the onion slices are completely covered. Set aside.

3. Add ground beef to a skillet and cook over medium-high heat, breaking it up as it cooks. Cook until the beef is done, with no remaining pink. Drain any excess fat.

4. Add remaining dried dill, a pinch of salt, oregano, and a pinch of pepper.

5. Increase heat to high and pour ⅔ cup of water into the skillet. Bring to a boil, reduce heat to low, and let it simmer until the water has evaporated.

6. To store in a fridge, add ½ cup of cooked pasta to a meal prep container, spoon some beef on top, add some red onion, hummus, and cucumber slices, drizzle with your yogurt sauce and Sriracha, and sprinkle with shredded Parmesan cheese. Serve with pita wedges.

CHICKEN CACCIATORE

Serves: 6

Prep time: 10 minutes

Cook time: 1½ hours

NUTRITION FACTS (PER SERVING)

Calories 683, Total Fat 27.6 g, Saturated Fat 6.9 g, Cholesterol 269 mg, Sodium 282 mg, Total Carbohydrates 12.4 g, Dietary Fiber 3 g, Total Sugars 7.9 g, Protein 90.9 g, Calcium 85 mg, Iron 6 mg, Potassium 1217 mg

INGREDIENTS:

2 Tbsp. extra-virgin olive oil

3½ lb. (1.6 Kg) chicken thighs

1 white onion (70 g), sliced

1 red bell pepper (120 g), sliced

8 oz. (225 g) button mushrooms, sliced

½ cup (90 g) olives

2 garlic cloves, sliced

⅓ cup (80 ml) white wine

1 (28-oz.) can plum tomatoes

2 tsp. fresh thyme, chopped

2 tsp. fresh oregano, chopped

Salt

Freshly ground black pepper

DIRECTIONS:

1. Heat the Dutch oven / cooking pot with olive oil over medium heat.

2. Cook the chicken pieces in batches, skin-side down, for 5 minutes on each side or until evenly browned. Put them on a platter and repeat for the remaining chicken.

3. Pour in the 2 tablespoons of olive oil. Put onion slices, mushrooms, and peppers in the pot and turn the heat to high.

4. Cook frequently stirring for 10 minutes or until the onions are translucent. Add garlic and cook for 1 minute.

5. Add wine and use a spoon to scrape the browned pieces at the bottom of the pot. Simmer to reduce the wine by half.

6. Add tomatoes and olives. Stir in chopped oregano and thyme. Season with salt and pepper. Simmer for 5 minutes while uncovered.

7. Put the chicken pieces in the tomato sauce. Use a lid to partially cover and lower the heat.

8. Simmer while occasionally basting and turning until the chicken is ready, or for 30-40 minutes.

9. Store in a fridge for 4-5 days. Serve warm with your favorite sides.

ARROZ VALENCIANA WITH CHORIZO

Serves: 8

Prep time: 10 minutes

Cook time: 1 hour 30 minutes

NUTRITION FACTS (PER SERVING):

Calories 491, Total Fat 12.5 g, Saturated Fat 3.6 g, Cholesterol 121 mg, Sodium 284 mg, Total Carbohydrates 41.8 g, Dietary Fiber 1.6 g, Total Sugars 1.6 g, Protein 50.5 g, Calcium 34 mg, Iron 4 mg, Potassium 137 mg

8 chicken thighs (420 g), skinless, boneless

Salt

Freshly ground black pepper

2½ Tbsp. extra-virgin olive oil

1 white onion (70 g), chopped

3 cloves garlic, minced

2 cups (420 g) long-grain rice

2 tsp. ground cumin

2 tsp. dried oregano

5 cups (1.2 L) low-sodium chicken broth or stock

1 bell pepper (120 g), diced

1¾ cups (420 ml) tomato puree

¾ lb. (340 g) spicy chorizo chicken sausages, diced

6 - 8 sprigs cilantro leaves, for garnish

¼ cup chopped scallions, for garnish

6 - 8 lime wedges, for garnish

DIRECTIONS:

1. Preheat the oven to 350℉ (177℃). Season chicken with salt and pepper.

2. Heat the olive oil in a Dutch oven over medium heat. Place half of the chicken pieces, and fry for about 3 minutes. Turn the chicken over and cook for 3 minutes until it is lightly browned on both sides. Transfer the chicken to a platter, and repeat it

3. Pour more oil into the pot, and add chopped onion. Cook until softened. Add minced garlic and cook for 2 minutes, or until softened.

4. Add rice, cumin, oregano, and some salt, and cook for 2 - 3 minutes, stirring until the rice is coated with oil. Stir in broth. Add green peppers and salsa. Bring to a boil.

5. Cover, put in the preheated oven, and bake for 30 minutes until the liquid is completely absorbed.

6. Stir in chorizo. Tuck the chicken pieces into the rice mixture, and pour in any juices collected on the platter. Cover, place in the oven again, and cook for 20 minutes until the chicken is cooked and the rice is tender.

7. Garnish with cilantro leaves, chopped scallions, and lime wedges.

8. Store in meal prep containers in a fridge for 4-5 days.

CHICKEN PENNE PASTA

Serves: 5 | Prep time: 10 min. | Cook time: 45 min.

½ lb. (225 g) penne pasta, cooked

3 Tbsp. extra-virgin olive oil, divided

1 white onion (70 g), chopped

3 cloves garlic, minced

3 bunches kale (21 oz./600 g), shredded

Salt

Freshly ground black pepper

1½ cups (210 g) cooked chicken, shredded

1 cup (120 g) Gruyere cheese, grated

1 lemon, juiced

¼ cup (30 g) Parmesan cheese, grated

¼ cup (15 g) panko crumbs

DIRECTIONS:

1. Preheat an oven to 375°F (190°C). Heat 2 tablespoons of olive oil in a Dutch oven over medium heat. Cook onion until translucent or about 5 minutes.

2. Add garlic and sauté for 30 seconds. Add kale to the pot and season with salt and pepper. Stir a few times to wilt the greens.

3. Close the lid, reduce heat to medium-low, and cook until the greens are tender for about 10 minutes.

4. Add the pasta, chicken, shredded Gruyere, and lemon juice to the greens, and season with salt and pepper.

5. In a small bowl, combine grated Parmesan, panko crumbs, and the remaining 1 tablespoon of olive oil. Pour the mixture over the top of the pasta, and place in the heated oven, uncovered, for 30 minutes, or until the top becomes slightly golden.

NUTRITION FACTS (PER SERVING):

Calories 569, Total Fat 21.5 g, Cholesterol 176 mg, Total Carbohydrates 33.8 g, Dietary Fiber 1.2 g, Sugars 2.3 g, Protein 58.4g

PAN-FRIED SALMON WITH VEGETABLES

Serves: 2

Prep Time: 15 min.

Cook Time: 15 min.

INGREDIENTS:

8 oz. (225 g) salmon fillets

1 tsp. dried basil

½ tsp. red pepper flakes

2 garlic cloves, minced

1 cup (100 g) cauliflower florets

1 cup (90 g) broccoli florets

2 Tbsp. extra virgin olive oil

a handful of fresh basil

1 Tbsp. lemon juice

10 pitted olives

2 Tbsp. hummus

salt

black pepper

DIRECTIONS:

1. Rub salmon with dried basil, 1 minced garlic clove, and red pepper flakes.

2. Heat olive oil in a nonstick pan. Add broccoli, cauliflower, lemon juice, basil, and the rest of the minced garlic. Season with salt and pepper and cook for 2 min.

3. Transfer the vegetables to a plate and add the salmon to the pan, cooking over medium-high heat. Cover with a lid and cook for 6–7 min., flipping the salmon halfway through.

4. Arrange your salad. Place vegetable mixture in a bowl, add olives and hummus and top it off with the salmon. Sprinkle with fresh basil.

5. Spread into containers and store in a fridge for 3-4 days.

NUTRITION FACTS (PER SERVING):

Calories: 580, Carbohydrates: 20 g, Protein: 38 g, Fat: 40 g, Fiber: 8 g, Sugar: 4 g

LEMON BASIL CREAM PASTA

Serves: 4

Prep Time: 10 min.

Cook Time: 15 min.

NUTRITIONAL FACTS/INFO (PER SERVING):

Calories: 527, Carbohydrates: 66 g, Protein: 16 g, Fat: 25 g, Fiber: 10 g, Sugar: 9 g

INGREDIENTS:

4 oz. (100 g) arugula

1 cup (135 g) peas

3 cups (270 g) broccoli florets

1 medium onion (70 g), diced

2 Tbsp. extra virgin olive oil

sea salt and black pepper

3 oz. (85 g) cherry tomatoes/sun-dried tomatoes, halved

8 oz. (220 g) whole wheat cannelloni pasta

Sauce:

1 cup (60 g) fresh basil

1 cup (140 g) roasted cashews

3 garlic cloves

½ lemon, juiced

½ tsp. sea salt

1 cup (240 ml) water

DIRECTIONS:

1. Cook your pasta according to the package directions. Just before the pasta is done, add in the broccoli florets as it finishes cooking. Take out 1 cup of the pasta water, drain, and set aside.

2. While the pasta is cooking, prepare your sauce. Combine all the ingredients in your blender until there are no lumps.

3. Heat the oil in a large skillet on medium heat to cook your vegetables. Sauté the bell peppers and onion with the seasonings until tender. Mix in the sun-dried tomatoes and arugula, cooking until it wilts slightly.

4. When all the ingredients are ready, toss the pasta and broccoli with the vegetables. Coat the dish with your sauce and add some pasta water until your desired consistency is met.

5. The components can be stored in the refrigerator for up to 1 week. Preferably, add the arugula when reheating.

SALAD WITH LENTILS AND VEGETABLES

Serves: 4

Prep Time: 10 min.

Cook Time: 20 min.

NUTRITION FACTS (PER SERVING):

Calories: 208, Carbohydrates: 19 g, Protein: 7 g, Fat: 13 g, Fiber: 6 g, Sugar: 4 g

INGREDIENTS:

1⅓ cups (260 g) lentils, soaked

3 cherry tomatoes (50 g), chopped

3 garlic cloves, sliced

2 garlic cloves, minced

3 Tbsp. extra virgin olive oil

½ tsp. cumin

½ tsp. coriander

½ tsp. turmeric

1 tsp. mint

1 tsp. red pepper flakes

½ white onion (35 g), chopped

a handful of spinach

salt

1 Tbsp. tahini

1 lime, juiced

1 medium cucumber, diced

2 tomatoes (240 g), diced

1 white onion (70 g), diced

DIRECTIONS:

1. Add diced cucumber, tomatoes, onion, and 1 tablespoon of olive oil to a bowl, and mix well. Set aside.

2. Cook your chopped onion, 1 tablespoon of olive oil, and 2 sliced garlic cloves in a pan over medium-high heat. Add spices and chopped tomato. Smash the tomato with a spatula after a few minutes of cooking.

3. Stir in lentils. Season with salt and add about 1 cup of water to cover the lentil mixture completely. Cover with a lid and cook for 10–15 min.

4. Add spinach and cook for 5 minutes. Add more water if needed.

5. Turn off the heat and add the remaining sliced garlic clove and another tablespoon of olive oil.

6. Mix tahini, lime juice, minced garlic, and a pinch of salt in a small bowl. Add 2–3 tablespoons of water until you reach your desired creaminess.

7. Arrange the bowl, and store the leftovers separately.

MUSHROOM RISOTTO

Serves: 3

Prep time: 10 minutes

Cook time: 40 minutes

NUTRITION FACTS (PER SERVING):

Calories 684, Total Fat 12.3 g, Saturated Fat 8.7 g, Cholesterol 0 mg, Sodium 1603 mg, Total Carbohydrates 115.5 g, Dietary Fiber 7.6 g, Total Sugars 5.3 g, Protein 19.4 g, Calcium 88 mg, Iron 7 mg, Potassium 576 mg

INGREDIENTS:

¾ oz. (20 g) dried porcini mushrooms

1 oz. (30 g) dried shiitake mushrooms

5 cups (1.2 L) low-salt chicken broth

2 Tbsp. coconut oil

1 medium yellow onion (70 g), finely diced

½ tsp. Kosher salt

½ tsp. ground black pepper

2 cups (420 g) Arborio rice

⅓ cup (80 ml) dry white wine

1½ cups (200 g) frozen petite peas, thawed

1 Tbsp. balsamic vinegar

3 Tbsp. fresh mint, chopped

1½ tsp. fresh thyme, chopped

DIRECTIONS:

1. Place the porcini and the shiitake mushrooms in a large bowl; then pour 2 cups of boiling water. Let the mushrooms soak for about 20 minutes. Pat them dry with a clean paper towel.

2. Transfer the mushrooms to a cutting board; discard any stems off them, then set them aside.

3. In a Dutch oven/cooking pot, heat the oil and toss the chopped onion with a pinch of salt and a pinch of fragrant ground black pepper. Sauté your ingredients for about 3 minutes.

4. Add rice and sauté for about 2 minutes. Add mushrooms and cook for about one minute. Add in dry wine and stir for 2 minutes.

5. Pour in chicken broth and close the lid.

6. Cook for 20 - 25 minutes on medium-high heat.

7. When the time is up, add in cooked peas and vinegar.

8. Add the thyme and mint; then season your risotto with a pinch of salt and a pinch of ground black pepper.

9. Transfer your risotto to meal prep containers and store it in a fridge.

10. Eat warm. Garnish with thyme and mint.

ROOT VEGETABLE HASH WITH SCRAMBLED EGGS

Serves: 2

Prep time: 10 min.

Cook time: 50 min.

NUTRITION FACTS (PER SERVING):

Calories 404, Total Fat 41.6 g, Saturated Fat 12.7 g, Cholesterol 402 mg, Sodium 631 mg, Total Carbohydrates 18 g, Dietary Fiber 3.4 g, Total Sugars 9.5 g, Protein 18.2 g, Calcium 183 mg, Iron 4 mg, Potassium 588 mg

INGREDIENTS:

1 very small red beet (50 g)

1 tiny (50 g) sweet potato

1 small (100 g) Yukon Gold potato

1 medium carrot (60 g)

½ medium onion (35 g), coarsely chopped

3 Tbsp. olive oil

¼ tsp. kosher salt, plus more for sprinkling

1 Tbsp. salted butter

4 large eggs

Freshly ground black pepper

¼ cup (30 g) Parmesan, grated

DIRECTIONS:

1. Preheat an oven to 375°F (190°C).

2. Peel the beet, sweet potato, gold potato, and carrot, and cut them into approximately ½-inch pieces.

3. Add the cut vegetables and chopped onion to the Dutch oven and drizzle with olive oil to coat all the vegetables. Sprinkle with salt and toss to coat. Smooth the vegetables into an even layer.

4. Put the uncovered pot in the preheated oven and roast for 20 minutes. Remove the Dutch oven and stir the vegetables. Put to the oven again, roast for 15 minutes more, and stir again. Check one of the beet chunks with a small knife or fork to see if it is tender, or continue cooking for 10 to 15 minutes, if needed. The vegetables should be crisp on the outside but soft inside.

5. Put the Dutch oven on the stovetop over medium-low heat and move the hash to the perimeter of the pot. Add the butter to the center of the Dutch oven.

6. In a small bowl, whisk together the eggs with the remaining ¼ teaspoon of salt while the butter melts. When it is foaming, pour the eggs in and let sit for 30 seconds or so, just until they start to set. Stir the eggs for 1 - 2 minutes.

7. Store the hash in meal prep containers in a fridge.

8. Sprinkle the eggs and vegetables with pepper and cheese, and mix the eggs into the vegetables or serve them separately.

BEEF BOURGUIGNON

Serves: 8

Prep time: 30 min.

Cook time: 3 - 3½ hours

NUTRITION FACTS (PER SERVING):

Calories 553, Total Fat 54 g, Saturated Fat 21.5 g, Cholesterol 175 mg, Sodium 1011 mg, Total Carbohydrates 46 g, Dietary Fiber 4.8 g, Total Sugars 16.9 g, Protein 52.8 g, Calcium 148 mg, Iron 10 mg, Potassium 1865 mg

2½ lb. (1.25 Kg) chuck beef, cut into 1-inch cubes

Salt

Freshly ground black pepper

¾ cup (100 g) gluten-free flour (made from fava beans or garbanzo beans), divided

4 Tbsp. extra-virgin olive oil

6 oz. (170 g) applewood-smoked bacon, diced

8 red onions (560 g), diced

12 baby carrots, halved

1 lb. (450 g) mushrooms, sliced

2 tbsp. salted butter

2 white onions (140 g), diced

6 cloves garlic, diced

2 Tbsp. tomato paste

½ tsp. dried thyme

1 (750-ml) bottle dry red burgundy wine

4 cups (960 ml) beef broth or stock

DIRECTIONS:

1. Preheat the oven to 325°F (163°C).

2. Sprinkle beef cubes with salt and pepper, then lightly coat with ½ cup of flour.

3. Heat olive oil in a Dutch oven over medium heat. Cook the bacon until fat is rendered. Transfer to a platter. Working in batches, sear the beef in the hot fat for 3 - 5 minutes, until brown on all sides. Transfer to the platter with the bacon, and continue searing until all the beef is browned.

4. Add red onions, carrots, and mushrooms to the pot and cook for 2 - 3 minutes. Transfer to a platter. Add salted butter to the pot. Put the onions and garlic, and cook for 4 - 5 minutes, or until transparent.

5. Stir in the remaining ¼ cup of flour, tomato paste, and thyme. Cook for 2 minutes. Deglaze the pot with the wine, and bring to a boil. Pour in the broth, and return to a boil.

6. Return the bacon and beef cubes to the pot. Bring to a boil. Cover, place in the heated oven, and cook for 2 - 2½ hours.

7. Return the red onions, carrots, and mushrooms to the pot. Cook for 30 minutes. Arrange stew with rice in meal prep containers. Keep in a fridge for 4-5 days.

JUICY CHICKEN WITH VEGETABLES

Servings: 6

Cooking time: 1½ hours

INGREDIENTS:

1 whole chicken (1.5 Kg), cut into small pieces

4 peeled potatoes (500 g), cut into large pieces

4 cherry tomatoes (70 g), halved

2 (70 g) red onions, peeled and sliced

1 cup (100 g) mushrooms, sliced

rosemary to taste

1 tsp. garlic powder

salt and pepper to taste

3 garlic cloves, peeled

2 Tbsp. salted butter

2 Tbsp. olive oil

½ cup (120 ml) water

DIRECTIONS:

1. Preheat the oven to 360℉ (182℃).

2. Rub chicken pieces with salt, pepper, and garlic powder.

3. Melt the butter in a pan and lightly fry all the chicken pieces until golden brown.

4. Slightly fry onion, garlic, and mushrooms in olive oil.

5. Put chicken, roasted vegetables, tomatoes, and potatoes into the Dutch oven. Pour ½ cup of water.

6. Close the Dutch oven with a lid and put it in a preheated oven for 45 minutes.

7. Remove from oven, sprinkle with finely chopped herbs.

8. Keep in a fridge. Serve warm.

NUTRITION FACTS (PER SERVING):

Calories 308, Total Fat 16 g, Saturated Fat 5.3 g, Cholesterol 37 mg, Sodium 161 mg, Total Carbohydrates 32 g, Dietary Fiber 4.9 g, Total Sugars 4.4 g, Protein 10.1 g, Vitamin D 45 mcg, Calcium 37 mg, Iron 2 mg, Potassium: 784 mg

MEDITERRANEAN PASTA

Serves: 6-8

Prep Time: 15 min.

Cook Time: 15 min.

INGREDIENTS:

6 garlic cloves, crushed

1 Tbsp. Mediterranean seasoning

2 cups (200 g) mushrooms, sliced

1 white onion (70 g), chopped

12 oz. (340 g) gluten-free fusilli pasta

1 Tbsp. red pepper flakes

1 Tbsp. sea salt

4 cups (120 g) fresh spinach

6 cherry tomatoes (110 g)

2 cups (340 g) white beans, cooked

DIRECTIONS:

1. Add pasta with 4 cups (960 ml) of water to your instant pot, set to high pressure, and cook for four minutes. Release the pressure carefully.

2. Rinse the pasta and set it aside.

3. Set your instant pot on the sauté function. Sauté olive oil, beans, garlic, mushrooms, onions, and spices for 10 min.

4. Stir in tomatoes and cook for 5 minutes. Once the vegetables are tender, you can blend a small amount to create a thicker sauce or leave everything as is.

5. Toss the pasta with the sauce, and you are ready to eat!

6. Keep in airtight containers for 3-4 days in the refrigerator.

NUTRITION FACTS (PER SERVING):

Calories: 353, Carbohydrates: 71 g, Protein: 16 g, Fat: 2 g, Fiber: 11 g, Sugar: 5 g

CHICKEN WITH GREEN BEANS

Serves: 2

Prep Time: 8 min.

Cook Time: 12 min.

NUTRITION FACTS (PER SERVING):

Calories: 352, Carbohydrates: 15 g, Protein: 24 g, Fat: 23 g, Fiber: 5 g, Sugar: 6 g

INGREDIENTS:

8 oz. (230 g) boneless, skinless chicken thighs (or chicken breast)

2 Roma tomatoes (300 g), chopped

4 oz. (115 g) green French beans, chopped

1 bell pepper (120 g), diced

1 tsp. tomato paste

1 carrot (60 g), chopped

½ cup (90 g) whole olives

2 garlic cloves

2 scallions

2 Tbsp. extra virgin olive oil

1 tsp dried basil (or a handful of chopped fresh basil)

½ tsp coriander

½ tsp red pepper flakes (optional)

DIRECTIONS:

1. Cut chicken into bite-sized pieces.

2. Heat olive oil in a skillet over medium-high heat.

3. Add your chicken and green beans, and cook for 4–5 min.

4. Add chopped tomatoes, cover with a lid, and cook for 3 min.

5. Stir in tomato paste. Add 1–2 tablespoons of water, if needed.

6. Reduce heat to medium. Stir in your scallions, bell pepper, carrots, basil (if you are using dried basil), coriander, and red pepper flakes (if using). Add 1 tablespoon of olive oil, and cook for 3–4 min.

7. Add olives, garlic, and basil (if you use fresh basil). Cook for 1 minute. Remove from heat.

8. Season with salt and pepper to taste, and serve. Store in airtight containers in a fridge for 4-5 days.

BAKED FISH WITH SEASONAL VEGETABLES

Serves: 6

Prep Time: 10 min.

Cook Time: 15 min.

NUTRITION FACTS (PER SERVING):

Calories: 128, Carbohydrates: 3.9 g, Protein: 21 g, Fat: 3 g, Fiber: 1.3 g

INGREDIENTS:

1½ lb. (675 g) white fish filet (such as halibut or cod)

salt

black pepper

extra virgin olive oil

1 lemon

8 oz. (230 g) cherry tomatoes

4 oz. (113 g) zucchini, chopped

1 small carrot (45 g), chopped

3 tbsp. red onion, diced

4–5 garlic cloves, minced

1 Tbsp. fresh thyme

2 tsp. dried oregano

DIRECTIONS:

1. Preheat the oven to 425°F (218°C). Brush a baking dish with olive oil.

2. Pat your fish dry with a paper towel. Season with salt and pepper all over.

3. Place the fish in the baking dish, and squeeze juice from half a lemon.

4. Mix tomatoes, chopped carrot, zucchini, onions, garlic, a pinch of salt and pepper, 3 tablespoons of olive oil, and spices in a bowl.

5. Pour the vegetable mixture over the fish.

6. Bake for 15–20 min. At the 15-minute mark, check if the fish is done by inserting a fork and twisting. If the fish easily flakes, it is done. Remove from the oven, and serve.

7. Store in airtight containers in a fridge.

GNOCCHI WITH MEDITERRANEAN VEGETABLES

Serves: 4

Prep Time: 10 min.

Cook Time: 20 min.

INGREDIENTS:

1 bag (16 oz./450 g) frozen gnocchi or cauliflower gnocchi

5 cups (650 g) bell peppers, diced

1 zucchini (320 g), quartered into bite-sized pieces

1 summer squash (200 g), quartered into bite-sized pieces

1 cup cherry tomatoes, halved

1 red onion (70 g), diced

½ lemon, juiced

2 Tbsp. avocado oil

1 tsp. salt

1 tsp. black pepper

DIRECTIONS:

1. Place an oven rack in the top position. Preheat your oven to 425°F (218°C). Line a large baking pan with foil.

2. Combine all ingredients, except the gnocchi, in a large bowl.

3. Transfer the mixture to the baking pan.

4. Add gnocchi, spreading everything out evenly.

5. Place the baking pan in the oven and roast for 10–15 minutes. Remove it from the oven, give it a stir, and then roast for another 5–10 minutes.

6. Turn your broiler on and broil for 3–5 min. Serve and enjoy.

7. Store in a fridge for 4-5 days.

NUTRITION FACTS (PER SERVING):

Calories: 220, Carbohydrates: 27.8 g, Protein: 4 g, Fat: 8.9 g, Fiber: 7.4 g

QUICHES & CASSEROLES

FRENCH QUICHE

Serves: 8

Prep Time: 15 min.

Cook Time: 55 min.

NUTRITION FACTS (PER SERVING):

Calories: 290, Carbohydrates: 20 g, Protein: 12 g, Fat: 19 g, Fiber: 3 g,
Sugar: 4 g

½ cup (60 g) sun-dried tomatoes

pie crust, cooked

2 Tbsp. unsalted butter

1 white onion (70 g), diced

2 garlic cloves, crushed

1 red bell pepper (120 g), diced

2 cups (60 g) fresh spinach

½ cup (50 g) mushrooms, sliced

1 tsp. dried oregano

1 tsp. dried parsley

⅓ cup (40 g) feta cheese, crumbled

4 medium eggs

1¼ cups (300 ml) whole milk

salt

black pepper

1 cup (120 g) cheddar cheese, shredded

DIRECTIONS:

1. Boil a small pot of water. Place sundried tomatoes in a glass measuring cup. Pour your boiling water over them so that they are just covered. Let them sit for 5 min. Drain and chop.

2. Preheat your oven to 375°F (190°C). Place a pie crust on a pie plate. Flute the edges.

3. Melt butter in a skillet over medium-high heat. Add garlic and onion, and cook for 3 min., until the onions are tender. Add bell pepper and cook for 3 more minutes until the pepper is tender.

4. Add spinach, mushrooms, parsley, and oregano, and cook for 5 minutes until the spinach has wilted.

5. Remove from heat. Add in feta cheese and tomatoes. Mix everything well. Spread the spinach filling into the pie crust.

6. Whisk eggs, milk, salt, pepper, and ½ cup of cheese in a bowl. Pour the mixture over the spinach mixture. Sprinkle it with the rest of the cheddar. cheese

7. Bake for 50–55 min. The crust should be golden brown.

8. Remove the quiche from the oven, and let it cool for 10–15 minutes before serving. Cover the quiche in sealed containers and refrigerate for 3-5 days.

CHICKEN, POTATO & BROCCOLI CASSEROLE

Serves: 6

Prep time: 10 min.

Cook time: 2 hours

INGREDIENTS:

Cooking spray

1 (15-oz./425 ml) can condensed cream of broccoli soup

1 cup (240 ml) sour cream

1½ cups (180 g) Swiss cheese, shredded

½ cup (120 ml) whole milk

6 cups (960 g) potatoes, cubed

3 cups (420 g) cooked chicken, chopped

1 teaspoon Italian seasoning

Salt

Freshly ground black pepper

2 cups (180 g) broccoli florets

¼ cup (15 g) fresh basil leaves, chopped

DIRECTIONS:

1. Preheat the oven to 350°F (177°C).

2. Lightly coat a Dutch oven with the cooking spray. Combine the broccoli soup and the sour cream. Stir in cheese, milk, chopped potatoes, chicken, and seasoning. Season with salt and pepper.

3. Cover with the lid, place in the heated oven and bake for 1 - 1½ hours.

4. Stir in the broccoli. Return to the oven and bake, uncovered, for 10 minutes. Stir in the basil and serve.

NUTRITION FACTS (PER SERVING):

Calories 743, Total Fat 40.6 g, Saturated Fat 24.1 g, Cholesterol 167 mg, Sodium 809 mg, Total Carbohydrates 40.6 g, Dietary Fiber 5 g, Total Sugars 6.3 g, Protein 53.4 g, Calcium 902 mg, Iron 2 mg, Potassium 985 mg

MUSHROOM SPINACH QUICHE

Serves: 6

Prep Time: 15 min.

Cook Time: 40 min.

NUTRITIONAL FACTS/INFO (PER SERVING):

Calories 223, Total Fat 9 g, Sodium 440 mg, Total Carbohydrates 46 g, Dietary Fiber 1 g, Total Sugars 1 g, Protein 11 g, Calcium 902 mg

INGREDIENTS:

14 oz. (400 g) block extra-firm tofu

5 cherry tomatoes (100 g), halved

8 oz. (220 g) cremini mushrooms, sliced

3 cups (90 g) fresh spinach, chopped

½ cup (90 g) green olives

1 tsp. salt

3 garlic cloves, minced

2 Tbsp. all-purpose flour

¾ tsp. garlic powder

½ tsp. onion powder

1-2 Tbsp. plain milk

2 Tbsp. extra virgin olive oil

1 small onion (50 g), chopped

½ tsp. turmeric

One 9-inch (22.5 cm) frozen pie shell thawed

DIRECTIONS:

1. Set your oven at 375°F (190°C) to preheat.

2. In a large pan, heat the oil over medium heat and add chopped onions. Sauté the onions until they are soft and gloriously browning. It should smell enticing and not like burned garlic.

3. Wilt the spinach in the pan and add some salt and black pepper if you'd like. Remove it from the heat and set it aside for now.

4. Crumble the tofu into a blender/food processor with the seasonings, flour, and half of the milk. Blend until the mixture is thick and creamy. If it comes out too thick, add in the remaining milk.

5. Fold the tofu mixture with the vegetable mixture in a separate bowl and then pour it into the pie crust.

6. Place the tomatoes and olives on top of the quiche by pressing down on them slightly. Bake for 30-40 minutes until you can see the heavenly golden coloring on top. Allow to cool slightly before enjoying it!

7. Cover the quiche in sealed containers and refrigerate for 3-5 days.

TOMATO QUICHE

Servings: 8

Prep Time + Cook Time: 3 hours

Program: DOUGH

NUTRITION FACTS (PER SERVING)

Calories 485; Total Fat 22.3 g, Saturated Fat 13 g, Cholesterol 99 mg, Sodium 415 mg, Total Carbohydrates 57.2 g, Dietary Fiber 9 g, Total Sugars 7.5 g, Protein 19.9 g, Vitamin D 8 mcg, Calcium 274 mg, Iron 4 mg, Potassium 542 mg

For sponge:

4/5 cup (200 ml) whole milk

⅓ cup (80 ml) lukewarm water

2 cups (250 g) whole grain flour

2 tsp. (5 g) fresh yeast

For dough:

2 Tbsp. (40 g) liquid honey

¼ cup (60 g, ½ stick) butter

2 cups (250 g, 8 oz.) all-purpose flour

2½ Tbsp. (25 g) fresh yeast

¼ tsp. salt

After beeping:

1 cup (100 g) sun-dried tomatoes, chopped

For filling:

0.9 lb. (400 g) fresh tomatoes, sliced

For fill:

1 cup (100 g, 3 oz.) parmesan

½ cup (50 g) Gouda cheese

1¼ cups (300 ml) sour cream

2 whole eggs, slightly beaten

pizza spicy mix

black pepper, salt to taste

DIRECTIONS:

1. Put all ingredients for the bread starter into the bread machine and start the program DOUGH. Also, you can knead the sponge by hand. When the components have mixed well, stop the program. Let the dough rest and rise for 30 minutes.

2. Then add the dough ingredients. Set DOUGH mode again. Or do it by hand as well. Let the dough rest and rise for 45 minutes.

3. Combine all the ingredients for the fill.

4. Take the dough out of the bread maker, roll it out evenly, and place it (forming a board) on a baking sheet covered with oiled parchment paper.

5. Cover with tomato slices and pour filling over the dough.

6. Let the pie rest and rise in a warm place for 30 minutes.

7. Preheat the oven to 400°F (205°C). Bake until golden brown (about 25-30 minutes).

8. Cover the quiche in sealed containers and refrigerate for 4 days.

BREAKFAST CASSEROLE

Serves: 8

Prep Time: 15 min.

Cook Time: 30 min.

NUTRITION FACTS (PER SERVING):

Calories: 136, Carbohydrates: 4.2 g, Protein: 7.8 g, Fat: 10.2 g, Fiber: 1.1 g

1 red bell pepper (120 g), chopped

1 small zucchini (250 g), diced

2 green onions, chopped

4 oz. (113 g) broccoli florets

1 small red onion (50 g), diced

salt

black pepper

4 Tbsp. extra virgin olive oil

7 medium eggs

¼ tsp. baking powder (optional)

¼ cup (60 ml) plain milk

⅓ cup (40 g) crumbled feta cheese, plus more for serving

⅓ cup chopped parsley, plus more for serving

1 tsp. fresh thyme

DIRECTIONS:

1. Preheat your oven to 450°F (230°C). Place a rimmed baking sheet in the oven and let it heat up a bit.

2. Mix bell peppers, red onion, zucchini, green onion, broccoli, 3 tablespoons olive oil, and a pinch of salt and black pepper in a bowl.

3. Remove the pan from the oven and arrange your veggie mixture on the pan. Place the pan back in the oven and cook for 15 min. Remove the veggies from the oven. Lower your heat to 400°F (205°C).

4. Whisk together eggs, baking powder (if using), milk, feta, parsley, thyme, and a pinch of salt and black pepper.

5. Add the veggies to the egg mixture, folding them in.

6. Pour your mixture into the casserole dish and transfer it to the oven. Cook for 8–10 minutes. Remove from the oven. Sprinkle with feta and parsley.

PEAR CHEESE QUICHE

Servings: 8

Prep Time + Cook Time: 2 hours

Program: DOUGH

NUTRITION FACTS (PER SERVING)

Calories 559; Total Fat 22.6 g, Saturated Fat 11.2 g, Cholesterol 91 mg, Sodium 873 mg, Total Carbohydrates 70.4 g, Dietary Fiber 13.5 g, Total Sugars 13.4 g, Protein 26.9 g, Vitamin D 4 mcg, Calcium 300 mg, Iron 3 mg, Potassium 485 mg

For dough:

1¼ cup (300 ml) lukewarm water

3 Tbsp. olive oil

3½ cups (500 g, 15¾ oz.) whole grain flour

¼ tsp. sea salt

1 package active dry yeast

For filling:

5 pears (1 Kg)

5 Tbsp. lemon juice

1¾ cup (400 g) Gorgonzola cheese

1⅓ cup (300 g) cottage cheese

4 Tbsp. apple cider vinegar

2 whole eggs

ground nutmeg

2 garlic cloves, crushed

pepper, salt to taste

DIRECTIONS:

1. Knead the dough in a bread machine or by hand. Let it rest for 45 minutes.

2. Peel the pears and cut them into halves. Remove the cores, and then sprinkle the pears with lemon juice. Put them in a saucepan, cover with boiling water, cover with a lid, and cook for 5 minutes on low heat. Take the pears out and let them drain to dry.

3. In another bowl, mash gorgonzola with a fork, add full-fat cottage cheese and crushed garlic, and season with salt, pepper, and nutmeg. Stir in the eggs.

4. Take the dough out of the bread maker, roll it out evenly, and place it (forming a board) on a baking sheet covered with oiled parchment paper.

5. Cut the pear halves into thin slices and evenly lay them onto the dough surface. Spread the cheese mixture over the pears.

6. Leave in a warm place for 30 minutes to rest and rise.

7. Preheat the oven to 400°F (205°C).

8. Bake the tart for 25-30 minutes (until golden brown).

VEGETABLE POLENTA CASSEROLE

Serves: 8

Prep time: 20 min.

Cook time: 1½ hours

NUTRITION FACTS (PER SERVING):

Calories 921, Total Fat 6.2 g, Saturated Fat 0.9 g, Cholesterol 1 mg, Sodium 69 mg, Total Carbohydrates 170.4 g, Dietary Fiber 47.6 g, Total Sugars 12 g, Protein 50.1 g, Calcium 294 mg, Iron 16 mg, Potassium 2609 mg

INGREDIENTS:

2 (19-oz./540 g) cans white kidney beans, rinsed and drained

1 (19-oz./540 g) can garbanzo beans, rinsed and drained

1 cup (200 g) white onion, chopped

4 garlic cloves, minced

1 tsp. dried thyme

1 tsp. dried oregano

1 (16-oz./450 g) tube refrigerated cooked polenta, cut into ½-inch (1.3 cm) slices

2 cups (240 g) assorted Italian cheeses, shredded

1 large tomato (150 g), diced

2 cups (60 g) fresh spinach leaves

DIRECTIONS:

1. Preheat the oven to 325°F (163°C).

2. Mix the kidney beans, garbanzo beans, onion, garlic, thyme, and oregano in a large bowl.

3. In a Dutch oven, layer half of the bean mixture, half of the polenta, and half of the cheeses. Add the remaining bean mixture and the remaining polenta.

4. Cover, place in the preheated oven, and cook for 1 - 1½ hours.

5. Remove the pot from the oven. Uncover and sprinkle the remaining cheeses on top. Add the tomato and spinach, toss lightly, and serve.

6. Store in a fridge for 3-5 days.

PROSCIUTTO PEAR QUICHE

Servings: 8

Prep Time + Cook Time: 2 hours

Program: DOUGH

NUTRITION FACTS (PER SERVING)

Calories 720; Total Fat 32.7 g, Saturated Fat 12.9 g, Cholesterol 80 mg, Sodium 1616 mg, Total Carbohydrates 77.9 g, Dietary Fiber 11.3 g, Total Sugars 19 g, Protein 32.8 g, Vitamin D 2 mcg, Calcium 403 mg, Iron 3 mg, Potassium 606 mg

For dough:

1 cup (240 ml) lukewarm water

½ cup (120 ml) buttermilk

3½ cups (500 g, 15¾ oz.) whole grain flour

¼ tsp. sea salt

1 package active dry yeast

For filling:

4 pears (700 g)

2 Tbsp. salted butter

1 tsp. ground chili

1 tsp. liquid honey

2 cups (200 g) Roquefort cheese, grated

Salt, and pepper to taste

For fill:

2 cups (500 ml) Greek yogurt

1¼ cup (300 ml) mayonnaise

½ cup (50 g) parmesan cheese

1 Tbsp. mustard

10 slices (170 g) Prosciutto di Parma ham

DIRECTIONS:

1. Knead the dough in a bread machine or by hand. Let it rest for 45 minutes.

2. To make the topping, wash and peel the pears, cut them into strips, and roast them in a buttered frying pan with chili pepper, honey, salt, and black pepper. Let the mixture cool down.

3. Take the dough out of the bread maker, roll it out evenly, and place (forming a board) on a baking sheet covered with oiled parchment paper.

4. Evenly spread the pear filling and cover with Roquefort cheese. Cover with slices of ham.

5. Leave in a warm place for 30 minutes to rest and rise.

6. Preheat the oven to 400℉ (205℃).

7. For the fill, combine yogurt, mayonnaise, parmesan, and mustard. Cover the quiche.

8. Bake the quiche for 25-30 minutes (until golden brown).

BUCKLING GREEK VEGGIE CASSEROLE

NUTRITION FACTS (PER SERVING):

Calories: 163, Total Fat: 11 g, Saturated Fat: 1 g, Cholesterol: 16 mg, Sodium: 214 mg, Total Carbohydrate: 14 g, Dietary Fiber: 3 g, Total Sugar: 4 g, Protein: 4 g, Vitamin D: 0 mcg, Calcium: 114 mg, Iron: 2 mg, Potassium: 364 mg

INGREDIENTS:

¼ cup (30 g) feta cheese, crumbled

2 Tbsp. fresh dill, chopped

1 Tbsp. oregano, dried

1 Tbsp. fresh lemon juice

4 garlic cloves, sliced

1 lb. (450 g) sweet potatoes, cut into 1-inch wedges

½ lb. (225 g) green beans, trimmed

1 can (14 oz./400 g) whole tomatoes, peeled, quartered with juices

1 zucchini, 8 oz. (230 g), coarsely chopped

1 small onion (50 g), cut into ½-inch wedges

4 Tbsp. olive oil, divided

Salt as needed

DIRECTIONS:

1. Preheat your oven to 450°F (230°C).

2. Take a medium bowl, add onion, zucchini, and 1 tablespoon of olive oil, and toss well. Season with salt. Transfer to a large baking dish and roast for 12-15 minutes until zucchini is about to brown. Transfer zucchini and onion to a wire rack.

3. Add 3 tablespoons of oil, green beans, potatoes, tomatoes (with juice), lemon juice, garlic, and oregano to another medium bowl and stir. Season with salt.

4. Transfer the mixture to the same baking dish and top with roasted onion and zucchini.

5. Cover with foil and bake for 30 minutes. Remove foil and stir veggies.

6. Keep baking for about 25-35 minutes until the potatoes are tender and slightly brown.

7. Sprinkle dill on top and let it sit for about 10 minutes. Spread in meal prep containers and keep in a fridge.

SAUCES & DRESSINGS

GREEK LABNEH

Serves: 8 | Prep Time: 15 min. | Total Time: 12 hours

INGREDIENTS:

4 cups (960 ml) low-fat Greek yogurt

¼ tsp. salt

¼ cup (45 g) shelled pistachios

1 Tbsp. extra virgin olive oil

1 Tbsp. fresh parsley, chopped

1 tsp. lemon zest

¼ tsp. ground sumac

DIRECTIONS:

1. Line a large mesh sieve with four layers of cheesecloth. Place it over a deep bowl so that you have 3 inches of space between the sieve and the bottom of the bowl.

2. Whisk yogurt and salt in a bowl. Transfer the mixture to the cheesecloth.

3. Refrigerate for 12–24 hours.

4. Discard the liquid that has drained into the bowl.

5. Sprinkle pistachios, olive oil, parsley, lemon zest, and sumac over your dip and serve.

6. Serve with Italian bread slices. Store in a fridge.

NUTRITION FACTS (PER SERVING):

Calories: 108, Carbohydrates: 8.3 g, Protein: 7 g, Fat: 5.3 g, Fiber: 0.4 g

PESTO SAUCE

Serves: 16 Tbsp. (1 cup)

Prep Time: 5 min.

INGREDIENTS:

2 cups (120 g) fresh basil

3 large garlic cloves

2 Tbsp. fresh lemon juice

3 Tbsp. pine nuts/walnuts

2-3 Tbsp. extra virgin olive oil

¼ tsp. pink salt

3-6 Tbsp. water

DIRECTIONS:

1. Add all your ingredients except oil and water to a blender/food processor. Blend them until it forms a loose paste.

2. Gradually add the oil (continuously pouring into the mixture) and scrape down the sides. Next, mix in 1 tablespoon of water at a time until the consistency you prefer is formed. Taste and adjust according to your liking.

3. Cover and store in the refrigerator for 1 week or freeze for longer.

NUTRITIONAL FACTS/INFO (PER SERVING):

Calories: 39, Carbohydrates: 1.3 g, Protein: 1 g, Fat: 4 g, Fiber: 1 g, Sugar: 0.2 g

VINAIGRETTE SALAD DRESSING

Serves: 12 | Prep Time: 5 min. | Total Time: 5 min.

INGREDIENTS:

¾ cup (180 ml) extra virgin olive oil

1 lemon, zested

1 lemon (about ¼ cup), juiced

¼ cup (60 ml) red wine vinegar

1 tsp. Dijon mustard

1 tsp. dried oregano

1 garlic clove, minced

¼ cup (30 g) feta, crumbled (optional)

salt to taste

black pepper

DIRECTIONS:

1. Place olive oil, lemon zest and juice, vinegar, mustard, oregano, and garlic in a jar.
2. Seal the jar and shake vigorously. Add your feta (if using), and shake again.
3. Season with salt and pepper to taste.

NUTRITION FACTS (PER SERVING):

Calories: 132, Carbohydrates: 1 g, Protein: 1 g, Fat: 14 g, Fiber: 1 g, Sugar: 1 g

PEPPER ROMESCO SAUCE

Serves: 2 cups

Prep Time: 5 min.

INGREDIENTS:

2 garlic cloves

2 Tbsp. fresh lemon juice

½ cup (75 g) Marcona almonds

1 (12 oz./340 g) jar drained roasted red peppers

2 small tomatoes (200 g)

½ tsp. smoked paprika

1 tsp. basil/parsley/oregano/chili flakes (optional)

DIRECTIONS:

1. Place your garlic, lemon juice, red peppers, and tomatoes into a food processor/blender. Blend your ingredients until combined.

2. Next, blend in the almonds and paprika until a smooth mixture forms.

3. Store your sauce in a covered container for up to 5 days in the fridge.

4. Serve with pasta, sandwiches, or spiralized vegetables.

NUTRITIONAL FACTS/INFO (PER SERVING):

Calories: 67, Carbohydrates: 2 g, Protein: 4 g, Fat: 4 g, Fiber: 1 g, Sugar: 1 g

SPICY YOGURT SAUCE

Serves: 12

Prep Time: 5 min.

Total Time: 5 min.

INGREDIENTS:

1 cup (240 ml) Greek yogurt

2 Tbsp. Sriracha

1 tsp. paprika

2 garlic cloves, peeled

¼ tsp. salt

¼ tsp. black pepper

DIRECTIONS:

1. Place garlic in a food processor to dice, and blitz it for 2–3 seconds.
2. Add Greek yogurt, paprika, Sriracha, salt, and pepper. Blitz for 2–3 more seconds.
3. Scrape your mixture off the sides of the food processor and blitz for 2 seconds.
4. Transfer to a bowl and store in a fridge.
5. Serve with burgers or chicken pieces.

NUTRITION FACTS (PER SERVING):

Calories: 11, Carbohydrates: 1 g, Protein: 2 g, Fat: 1 g, Fiber: 1 g, Sugar: 1 g

TAHINI LEMON GARLIC SAUCE

Serves: 8

Prep Time: 10 min.

Total Time: 10 min.

INGREDIENTS:

3 garlic cloves

½ cup (120 ml) tahini

¼ cup (60 ml) lemon juice

1 Tbsp. extra virgin olive oil

salt

black pepper

DIRECTIONS:

1. Mince your garlic in a food processor.

2. Add your tahini, extra virgin olive oil, and lemon juice to the food processor, and mince for 10 seconds.

3. Add 4 tablespoons of water to the food processor, processing 1 tablespoon at a time until the mixture reaches your desired consistency.

4. Season with salt and pepper to taste.

NUTRITION FACTS (PER SERVING):

Calories: 108, Carbohydrates: 4 g, Protein: 3 g. Fat: 10 g, Fiber: 1 g, Sugar: 1 g

EGGPLANT GARLIC DIP

Serves: 8

Prep Time: 20 min.

Cook Time: 40 min.

NUTRITION FACTS (PER SERVING):

Calories: 103, Carbohydrates: 5.7 g, Protein: 2.8 g, Fat: 8.2 g, Fiber: 2.1 g, Sugar: 2.8 g

INGREDIENTS:

1 lb. (450 g) eggplant (1 large eggplant), cut into 1-inch cubes

3 Tbsp. extra virgin olive oil

½ tsp. salt

½ cup (120 ml) Greek yogurt

2 Tbsp. tahini

2 tsp. lemon juice

¼ tsp. cumin

¼ tsp. black pepper

1 garlic clove, thinly sliced

DIRECTIONS:

1. Preheat an oven to 400°F (205°C). Line a baking sheet with foil.

2. Mix eggplant, 2 tablespoons of olive oil, and ¼ tsp salt together in a large bowl. Arrange the mixture on a baking sheet.

3. Roast for 20 min., mix everything up, and roast for 20 minutes more.

4. Remove from the oven and let it sit for 10 minutes.

5. Transfer the eggplant to a food processor and pulse 8–10 times, so the eggplant is finely chopped.

6. Transfer chopped eggplant to a bowl and add yogurt, tahini, lemon juice, cumin, pepper, and the rest of the salt. Mix well to combine.

7. Heat 1 tablespoon of oil in a skillet over medium-low heat. Add garlic slices and cook for about 4 minutes, so it is golden and just starting to get crispy.

8. Transfer toasted garlic with the oil to a small bowl, and let it sit for 2 minutes to cool off before transferring it to your eggplant dip.

SWEET SNACKS

PEAR CRISP

Serves: 2

Prep Time: 5 min.

Cook Time: 10 min.

INGREDIENTS:

2 tsp. cinnamon

salt

2½ Tbsp. coconut oil

1 tbsp. liquid honey, plus more for serving

1½ Tbsp. coconut, shredded

2 pears (360 g), cubed

½ cup (40 g) oats

¼ cup (40 g) nuts

DIRECTIONS:

1. Place oats, nuts, shredded coconut, honey, 1½ tablespoon of coconut oil, 1 tablespoon of water, 1 tablespoon of cinnamon, and a pinch or two of salt in a food processor. Process until it reaches the consistency of a crumble.

2. Heat ½ tablespoon coconut oil in a pan, and add your crumble. Cook for 5 minutes, stirring occasionally. Remove from heat.

3. Place the rest of the coconut oil, cinnamon, and pears in another pan and sauté for 3–4 min. over medium heat.

4. Place the pear mixture and crumble mixture in a bowl and drizzle with more honey.

NUTRITION FACTS (PER SERVING):

Calories: 488, Carbohydrates: 57 g, Protein: 7 g, Fat: 29 g, Fiber: 11 g, Sugar: 28 g

CHICKPEA SNACKS

Serves: 5 (about 50 crackers)

Prep Time: 15 min.

Cook Time: 20 min.

INGREDIENTS:

1 tsp. baking powder

1 cup (90 g) chickpea flour (garbanzo bean flour)

2 Tbsp. extra virgin olive oil

½ tsp. sea salt + extra

3 Tbsp. water

DIRECTIONS:

1. Set your oven temperature to 350°F (177°C) and line a baking sheet with parchment paper.

2. Combine all the ingredients in a large bowl until a dough forms into a ball.

3. Sprinkle a surface and the dough ball with flour. Roll the dough out to a ⅛ inch thick.

4. Cut the dough into shapes with a knife/pizza cutter (squares/rectangles). Use a wet fork to prick the tops and sprinkle with extra salt.

5. Place the shapes on the baking sheet and bake for 20 min. The crackers should be golden brown. Allow to cool.

6. Store the crackers at room temperature in airtight containers for 1 week.

NUTRITIONAL FACTS/INFO (PER SERVING):

Calories: 19, Carbohydrates: 2.5 g, Protein: 1 g, Fat: 0.8 g, Fiber: 0.7g, Sugar: 0.4 g

PLANT-BASED CHOCOLATE MOUSSE

Serves: 4

Prep Time: 5 min.

Cook Time: 10 min.

INGREDIENTS:

1¼ cups (300 ml) almond milk / coconut milk

1 lb. (450 g) dark chocolate, chopped

4 avocados (600 g), chopped

¼ cup (60 ml) agave syrup

1 Tbsp. orange zest

2 Tbsp. toasted almonds

2 tsp. sea salt

2 tsp. pepper flakes

1 Tbsp. extra virgin olive oil

DIRECTIONS:

1. Heat milk over medium-high heat in a saucepan until it reaches 175°F (80°C) on an instant-read thermometer. Remove from heat and stir in the chopped chocolate until it has melted. Set aside to cool.

2. Place avocados, agave syrup, orange zest, and cooled chocolate mixture in a blender. Blend on high until everything is smooth.

3. Serve and sprinkle with toasted almonds, sea salt, and pepper flakes. Drizzle with olive oil.

4. Store in Mason jars in a fridge.

NUTRITION FACTS (PER SERVING):

Calories: 596, Carbohydrates: 92 g, Protein: 26 g, Fat: 42 g, Sugar: 12g

ALMOND LEMON CAKE

Serves: 10

Prep Time: 1 hour 10 min.

Cook Time: 42 min.

NUTRITION FACTS (PER SERVING):

Calories: 444, Carbohydrates: 41.3 g, Protein: 8 g, Fat: 29 g, Fiber: 3.1g, Sugar: 27.3 g

INGREDIENTS:

2 cups (225 g) almond flour

¾ cup (100 g) polenta

1½ tsp. baking powder

¼ tsp. salt

4/5 cup (190 g) unsalted butter, plus more

1 cup (250 g) granulated sugar

3 medium eggs

2 lemons, zested

½ tsp. vanilla extract

½ cup (70 g) powdered sugar

3 Tbsp. lemon juice

whipped cream (optional, for serving)

DIRECTIONS:

1. Preheat an oven to 350℉ (177℃). Line a 9-inch (22.5 cm) round cake pan with parchment paper and coat with some butter.

2. Whisk almond flour, polenta, salt, and baking powder in a bowl.

3. Whisk granulated sugar and butter in a large bowl using an electric mixer. Beat for about 3 minutes.

4. Add ⅓ of the mixture to your butter mixture and continue to beat until everything is mixed well. Add an egg and continue to beat. Continue adding the flour mixture in thirds. Add lemon zest and vanilla extract and beat to combine.

5. Transfer your batter to the cake pan, spreading it out evenly.

6. Bake for 40 minutes, or until the cake's edges start to separate from the sides of the pan. Remove the cake from the oven and place it on a wire rack to cool.

7. Add powdered sugar and lemon juice to a saucepan over low heat. Cook, occasionally stirring, until the sugar is dissolved.

8. Use a toothpick to poke holes in the cake about 1 inch apart. Drizzle your syrup mixture all over the cake.

9. Cut your cake and serve with whipped cream (if using).

PLAIN HONEY CAKE

Serves: 12

Prep Time: 20 min.

Cook Time: 40 min.

INGREDIENTS:

1 cup (240 ml) Greek yogurt

⅔ cup (160 ml) extra virgin olive oil, plus more

⅔ cup (160 ml) honey

1 Tbsp. chopped thyme

1 tsp. lemon zest

3 medium eggs

1½ cups (200 g) all-purpose wheat flour

½ tsp. baking powder

½ tsp. baking soda

¼ tsp. salt

DIRECTIONS:

1. Heat an oven to 325°F (163°C). Line a 9-inch (22.5 cm) round cake pan with parchment paper and coat with some olive oil.

2. Whisk together yogurt, olive oil, honey, thyme, and lemon zest in a large bowl. Beat eggs in one at a time. Add wheat baking flour, baking powder, baking soda, and salt. Mix until the batter is almost smooth.

3. Spread the batter into the cake pan evenly.

4. Bake for 40–45 minutes, until the top of the cake's top is lightly browned. Use a toothpick to check if the cake is done by sticking it in the center of the cake. If it comes out clean, the cake is done. If it does not, let it bake for a few more minutes.

5. Transfer the cake to a cooling rack for 10 minutes before taking it out of the pan. Serve warm or at room temperature and top with berries.

NUTRITION FACTS (PER SERVING):

Calories: 260, Carbohydrates: 28.5 g, Protein: 5 g, Fat: 14.6 g, Fiber: 0.6 g, Sugar: 16.4 g

HOMEMADE BANANA COOKIES

Serves: 14 | Prep Time: 20 min. | Cook Time: 10 min.

½ cup (80 g) roasted and salted peanuts, chopped

2 Tbsp. sugar (optional)

1 cup (240 ml) chunky peanut butter

⅔ cup (120 g) coconut sugar

1 medium ripe banana (120 g), mashed

2 Tbsp. maple syrup

2 tsp. vanilla extract

½ tsp. baking soda

½ tsp. salt

DIRECTIONS:

1. Preheat your oven to 375°F (190°C). Line two baking sheets with parchment paper.

2. Chop peanuts. Set aside half of them, and keep chopping the rest until they are finely chopped. Place the finely chopped peanuts in a small bowl and add sugar (if using). Set aside.

3. Mix reserved coarsely chopped peanuts, peanut butter, salt, baking soda, vanilla, syrup, mashed banana, and coconut sugar in a bowl until the mixture is sticky and thick. Let it sit for 15 min.

4. Place one large scoop of dough into the bowl with the finely chopped peanuts and roll around to coat. Form the dough into a ball and place it on your baking sheet, flattening it into a thick cookie shape. Repeat for the rest of the dough.

5. Bake for 8–10 min. Let them cool for 10 minutes before serving.

Calories: 185, Carbohydrates: 18 g, Protein: 5 g, Fat: 11 g, Sugar: 15g

HOMEMADE PROTEIN DESSERT SNACKS

Serves: 8

Prep Time: 2¼ hours

INGREDIENTS:

2⅓ cups (400 g) dates, pitted

1⅓ cups (200 g) almonds

⅓ cup and ¼ cup of cocoa powder

2 tsp. vanilla extract

¼ tsp. sea salt

1 cup (140 g) dried cherries

1 cup (150 g) macadamia nuts, roughly chopped

¼ cup (60 ml) maple syrup

2 Tbsp. coconut oil, melted

DIRECTIONS:

1. Grease an 8-inch (20 cm) square baking pan and line it with parchment paper.

2. Add dates, almonds, ⅓ cup of cocoa powder, 1 tablespoon of water, vanilla extract, and salt to a food processor and process until everything is smooth. Spread out your mixture evenly into the pan.

3. Sprinkle dried cherries and macadamia nuts over everything and lightly press them into the batter.

4. Mix coconut oil, syrup, and ¼ cup of cocoa powder in a bowl. Pour the mixture over the batter, spreading it out evenly.

5. Place your pan in the fridge. Let it chill for at least 2 hours before serving.

NUTRITION FACTS (PER SERVING):

Calories: 592, Carbohydrates: 83 g, Protein: 10 g, Fat: 31 g, Sugar: 65g

MEDITERRANEAN BAKING

MINI BAGUETTES

Servings: 8 baguettes | Program: DOUGH

Prep Time + Cook Time: 2½ hours

INGREDIENTS:

1⅓ cup (320 ml) lukewarm water

3½ cups (500 g, 14½ oz.) all-purpose flour

1 package active dry yeast

½ teaspoon salt

DIRECTIONS:

1. Knead the dough in a bread machine or by hand. Let it rest for 45 minutes.

2. Place ready-to-use dough on a floured surface and divide it into 8 equal parts. Form sphere-like pieces and let them rest for 5 minutes. Shape each piece into a long baguette.

3. Put the baguettes on a baking sheet covered with oiled parchment paper. Cover with a towel, let them rest, and rise for 45 minutes.

4. Preheat an oven to 425°F (218°C).

5. Slightly sprinkle each baguette with flour and make 3-5 diagonal incisions with a sharp knife.

6. Bake the baguettes until golden brown for 10-12 minutes. Allow to cool down on the grid.

NUTRITION FACTS (PER SERVING)

Calories 232, Total Fat 0.7 g, Saturated Fat 0.1 g, Cholesterol 0 mg, Sodium 149 mg, Total Carbohydrates 48.3 g, Dietary Fiber 2 g, Total Sugars 0.2 g, Protein 7 g, Vitamin D 0 mcg, Calcium 10 mg, Iron 3 mg, Potassium 97 mg

OLIVE ROLLS

Servings: 16 rolls | Program: DOUGH

Prep Time + Cook Time: 2 hours 10 minutes

For dough:

1¼ cup (300 ml) lukewarm water

3 Tbsp. olive oil

3 cups (420 g, 13½ oz.) all-purpose flour

⅔ cup (100 g, 3 oz.) whole-grain flour

1½ Tbsp. active dry yeast

½ tsp. sea salt

For filling:

3 Tbsp. pine nuts, roasted

1 cup (180 g) black olives, pitted

2 Tbsp. olive oil

1 small onion (50 g), diced

1 tsp. dried oregano

For glaze:

1 egg yolk, slightly beaten

2 Tbsp. whole milk

DIRECTIONS:

1. Knead the dough in a bread machine or by hand. Let it rest and rise for 40 minutes.

2. Grind olives, onion, oregano, and pine nuts in a blender.

3. Roll out the dough into a rectangular layer 14x10 inches (35x25 cm), and evenly distribute the filling on the surface. Make a roll.

4. Use a sharp knife to cut it into round slices 1-inch (2.5 cm) thick.

5. Place the rolls on a baking sheet covered with oiled parchment paper. Brush them with the egg-milk mix. Let it rest for 30 minutes.

6. Preheat the oven to 425°F (218°C).

7. Bake in the oven until golden brown for 12-15 minutes.

CHEESE PEAR BRIOCHE

Servings: 12 buns

Prep Time + Cook Time: 3 hours + night

Program: DOUGH

For dough:

1/5 cup (50 ml) whole milk

5 whole eggs, slightly beaten

⅓ cup (60 g, 2.4 oz.) granulated sugar

3½ cups (500 g, 15¾ oz.) all-purpose flour

1½ tsp. active dry yeast

½ tsp. sea salt

After beeping:

1 cup (225 g, 8 oz.) frozen butter, diced

Filling:

1 pear (180 g), peeled and chopped

1⅓ cup (170 g) cream cheese

For glaze:

1 egg, whipped

DIRECTIONS:

1. Knead the dough in a bread machine or by hand. Take it out, wrap it with a kitchen film, and put it in the fridge overnight.

2. Before cooking the buns, place the dough in a warm place for 1 hour.

3. After that, cut the dough into 12 equal parts. Pinch a small piece of dough off each of the parts.

4. Shape the big and small dough pieces into spheres. Place the large spheres in buttered cupcake baking cups and press your finger against the middle of their tops to deepen a little.

5. Mix chopped pear with soft cheese. Make a deepening in the large dough sphere, put the filling inside the deepening, and cover it with the small sphere.

6. Cover with a towel and leave for 1 hour to rest and rise.

7. Preheat the oven to 350°F (177°C).

8. Brush the surface of your brioches with a whipped egg.

9. Bake in the preheated oven until golden brown for 15-20 minutes.

10. Cool the brioche down on the grid.

Calories 400, Total Fat 22.9 g, Cholesterol 138 mg, Carbohydrates 40 g, Dietary Fiber 1.9 g, Total Sugars 6.6 g, Protein 9.2 g,

COTTAGE CHEESE CROISSANTS

Servings: 12 rolls

Prep Time + Cook Time: 2½ hours

Program: DOUGH

For dough:

⅔ cup (160 ml) whole milk

1¼ cup (150 g) cottage cheese

¼ cup (60 g, 2 oz.) unsalted butter

1 whole egg

⅓ cup (60 g, 2.4 oz.) granulated sugar

4 cups (500 g, 18 oz.) all-purpose flour

1 tsp. vanilla sugar

1½ tsp. active dry yeast

½ tsp. sea salt

For glaze:

1 egg yolk, slightly beaten

2 Tbsp. whole milk

2 Tbsp. almonds, chopped

DIRECTIONS:

1. Knead the dough in a bread machine or by hand. Let it rest and rise for 45 minutes.

2. Roll out the ready-to-cook dough into a circle 16 inches (40 cm) in diameter and divide it into 12 triangular sectors. Roll each triangle up, starting with its wide edge.

3. Place the rolls on a baking sheet covered with oiled parchment paper and brush them with the glaze mix. Cover with a towel and let it rest for 30 minutes.

4. Preheat the oven to 400°F (205°C).

5. Bake in the preheated oven until golden brown for 15 minutes.

NUTRITION FACTS (PER SERVING)

Calories 239, Total Fat 5.6 g, Saturated Fat 3.1 g, Cholesterol 43 mg, Sodium 65 mg, Total Carbohydrates 39.1 g, Dietary Fiber 1.5 g, Total Sugars 6.2 g, Protein 7.9 g,

MINI FOCACCIA WITH OLIVES

Servings: 8 flatbreads

Prep Time + Cook Time: 2¼ hours

Program: DOUGH

For dough:

1¼ cup (300 ml) lukewarm water

3 Tbsp. olive oil

1 tsp. liquid honey

4 cups (500 g) all-purpose flour

1½ tsp. active dry yeast

½ tsp. sea salt

For filling:

4 tsp. olive oil

½ cup (100 g) black/green olives, pitted and chopped

½ cup (100 g) soft sheep cheese

coarse sea salt

DIRECTIONS:

1. Knead the dough in a bread machine or by hand. Let it rest and rise for 1 hour.

2. Divide the dough into 8 equal parts, then shape it into flat buns.

3. Place them on a baking sheet covered with oiled parchment paper.

4. Combine sheep cheese with finely chopped olives.

5. Evenly spread the filling on the flatbreads.

6. Sprinkle with olive oil and coarse salt.

7. Cover with a towel. Leave for 45 minutes to rest and rise.

8. Preheat the oven to 425°F (218°C).

9. Bake in the oven for 10-12 minutes, until golden brown.

NUTRITION FACTS (PER SERVING)

Calories 372, Total Fat 15.4 g, Saturated Fat 2.8 g, Cholesterol 11 mg, Sodium 248 mg, Total Carbohydrates 49.6 g, Dietary Fiber 2.3 g, Total Sugars 1 g, Protein 9.2 g, Vitamin D 0 mcg, Calcium 83 mg, Iron 4 mg, Potassium 91 mg

MEAT CALZONE

Servings: 8 calzones

Prep Time + Cook Time: 2⅓ hours

Program: DOUGH

For dough:

1¼ (300 ml) lukewarm water

3 Tbsp. olive oil

4 cups (500 g) all-purpose flour

1 tsp. active dry yeast

½ tsp. sea salt

For filling:

1 yellow onion (70 g), chopped

1 cup (200 g) ground meat

2 Tbsp. olive oil

Salt, black pepper

0.7 lb. (300 g) tomatoes, peeled & sliced

2 Tbsp. tomato paste

2 cups (200 g) feta cheese

4 Tbsp. (30 g) black olives, finely chopped

DIRECTIONS:

1. Knead the dough in a bread machine or by hand. Let it rest and rise for 40 minutes.

2. Fry onion with ground meat in olive oil. Add tomatoes, tomato paste, salt, and pepper. Allow to cool down.

3. Combine with cheese and olives.

4. Divide ready-to-use dough into 8 equal pieces and roll them out.

5. Put the filling on each calzone.

6. Carefully pinch the dough edges.

7. Brush the dough surface with olive oil.

8. Place calzones on a baking sheet covered with oiled paper. Let them rest for 30 minutes.

9. Preheat the oven to 425°F (218°C). Bake in the preheated oven for 20 minutes.

NUTRITION FACTS (PER SERVING)

Calories 434, Total Fat 16.9 g, Cholesterol 41 mg, Sodium 338 mg, Carbohydrates 53 g, Dietary Fiber 2.9 g, Total Sugars 3.5 g, Protein 17.5 g,

CHEESE GRISSINI

Servings: 25 grissini

Prep Time + Cook Time: 2 hours

Program: DOUGH

NUTRITION FACTS (PER SERVING)

Calories 63, Total Fat 2.3 g, Cholesterol 3 mg, Sodium 65 mg, Carbohydrates 7.9 g, Dietary Fiber 0.4 g, Sugars 0.1 g, Protein 2.6 g,

For dough:	**For filling:**
⅔ cup (150 ml) lukewarm water	1 cup (100 g) hard cheese, grated
2 Tbsp. olive oil	1 tsp. ground paprika
2 cups (250 g) all-purpose flour	1 tsp. cumin
1 tsp. active dry yeast	
½ tsp. sea salt	

DIRECTIONS:

1. Knead the dough in a bread machine or by hand. Let it rest and rise for 30 minutes.

2. Combine all the ingredients for the filling.

3. Roll out the dough to make a rectangular layer 16x10 inches (40x30 cm).

4. Evenly spread the filling onto the dough and slightly press it down.

5. Wrap ⅓ of the dough to the center and slightly press it down.

6. Now you have a plain piece of dough at the top. Spread or brush the topping to your taste over it.

7. Wrap the opposite ⅓ of the dough to the center and slightly press it down.

8. Use a sharp knife to cut the dough into ½-inch (1 cm) wide strips.

9. Twist each strip several times, carefully stretching it lengthwise.

10. Place breadsticks on a baking sheet covered with oiled parchment paper. Then let them rest for 20 minutes.

11. Preheat the oven to 425°F (218°C).

12. Bake in the preheated oven for 15-20 minutes.

FROM THE AUTHOR

My name is Linda Gilmore. I am a food journalist and an author. I am highly recognized for making culinary magic in my home kitchen. I am also a busy mom of two. This means I am always on the run and looking for any chance to save time and money. I am a foodie through and through at my core, and I have grown into an advocate for the Mediterranean lifestyle. With a passion for healthy living and first-hand knowledge of what it takes to stick to a successful lifestyle plan, I am prepared to be your guide throughout this journey.

The internet is full of all the information a person might need, but surfing for the right pieces takes a lot of time and effort. Looking for answers to my amateurish questions made me read through countless complex professional texts.

How much did I wish I'd had a book with simple step-by-step explanations? Perhaps, that is the main reason why I've written this one.

I hope this book lets you enjoy Mediterranean meal prepping at home!

OUR RECOMMENDATIONS

Vegan Meal Prep Cookbook: Plant-Based Meal Prep Recipes for Healthy Eating and Saving Time

Mediterranean Air Fryer Cookbook: Heart-Healthy Mediterranean Recipes for Cooking with Your Air Fryer

Copyright